ASPECTS OF
CULTURAL CHANGE

JOSEPH B. ACEVES, Editor

Aspects of Cultural Change

Aspects of Cultural Change

JOSEPH B. ACEVES, Editor

Southern Anthropological Society
Proceedings, No. 6

SOUTHERN ANTHROPOLOGICAL SOCIETY
Distributed by the University of Georgia Press
Athens 30601

SOUTHERN ANTHROPOLOGICAL SOCIETY

Founded 1966

Officers 1971-1972

Copyright © 1972 by
Southern Anthropological Society

ISBN: 0-8203-0286-4
LC: 74-190047

Printed in the United States

Contents

Preface

THE topic of the key symposium at the sixth annual meeting of the Southern Anthropological Society, held in Dallas, Texas, on April 1-3, 1971, was "Anthropological Approaches to Development and Change." The purpose of this symposium was to examine social and cultural change as a process that is increasingly planned and directed (for better or worse) and as an ethical or moral problem for anthropologists who are engaged in programs of planned change. With the exception of Joseph Aceves's introduction, all of the papers in this volume were presented at the symposium.

The success of the meeting can be attributed to Joseph Aceves, who served as program chairman and as organizer of the key symposium, and to his colleague Ben Wallace, who served as local arrangements chairman. Much credit must also be given to Leslie Jackson and to other students at Southern Methodist University who attended to many details at the meeting with genuine enthusiasm. Once again I want to thank Ralph Stephens, director of the University of Georgia Press, for supporting this series from its inception until the present time. I am again grateful to my wife Joyce for editorial assistance.

Charles M. Hudson
SAS Editor

Introduction

Joseph B. Aceves

VARIOUS estimates place between 60 and 70 percent of the human race on the fringe of the output sphere of modern industrial society where they receive few benefits of modern technology and where they have little say in establishing the norms and priorities that affect the course of their lives. These societies, or segments of societies, once labeled "backward" and now more euphemistically called "developing" or "emerging," are poorly equipped to cope with the rapid transitions of modern technology and its attendant social transformations and, as a partial consequence, are viewed with disdain, ignored entirely, or engulfed into the spheres of influence of more powerful societies. A vital question that emerges out of this imbalance is how these "peripheral" societies or groups can adapt to the ideas, values, and organizational modifications necessary for them to participate more equitably in the fruits of "progress" without, at the same time, suffering the complete destruction of their own cherished values, identities, and cultures. For all the concern expressed over the plight of these "developing" or "emerging" groups, for all the money and effort spent, and for all the words of outrage, blame, and self-serving righteousness put forth in the media and at scholarly gatherings, what do we anthropologists know about change? And, granted our limited and imperfect knowledge, what can we do or, perhaps more importantly, what—if anything—should we do about it?

In the success-oriented, competitive rush of industrialized society, most people take it for granted that modernization through planning is a good thing. The acquisition of material possessions, upward social mobility, and the accumulation of "the good things in life" are all deeply embedded in the consciousness of the individual through the efforts of the various entities charged with his socialization. To the citizen of the United States, progress is a "good thing"; in the words of one of our major corporations, it is "our most important product."

1

Perhaps the greatest difference between us (the technological elite) and them (choose your own euphemism) is that we take change, even rapid social change, virtually as a given.

There is no weakening of the spirit of progress in the United States. The search for progress is not hampered by the lack of a will for action so much as by an uncertainty as to the proper modes of action. Perhaps motivated by a fear of randomness and chaos and by a belief in the rationality of man, we, the technological elite, accept the notion that changes should be brought about in a systematic manner designed to maximize benefits and minimize expenditures. Hence, planning for change assumes great importance. It is our conceit that planning is a "good thing"; our system of values and the exigencies of the real world as we perceive it demand that time, effort, and resources be used so effectively as to minimize the chances of failure. We have, in our modern industrial society, a low tolerance for those who fail.

At the heart of all planning is an underlying assumption that willful acts by some person or group are, and can be, directly responsible for transforming situation A into situation B. When situation B is regarded as being a state somehow superior or better than its predecessor, situation A, we are apt to label this result progress. Progress may refer to events such as improved crop yields, decreases in the morbidity rate, or the erection of high rise apartments for slum dwellers. It may also be used in reference to changes that are essentially trivial: the automobile tail fin, for example. In 1950 Cadillac automobiles appeared with two bumps, two shy metallic extrusions, at the end of each rear fender. Automobile designers and advertisers claimed that this made the vehicle more "aerodynamically stable" and this, of course, was supposed to be progress. Other manufacturers followed suit until the zenith was achieved: the 1957 Dodge. No longer was the tail fin shy and adolescent; it was now mature, blatant, and adorned with lights and reflectors so that no one could ignore it. Public acceptance and enthusiasm was overwhelming. Here was the American masculine ideal made incarnate in sheet metal; here was the epitome of power, mobility, prestige, and sexuality adorned by gigantic mammarian stigmata. Here was the Great American Tit On Wheels, and *that*, in a society where power, wheels, and bosoms were fetishes, represented progress with a vengeance.

Progress is not solely to be measured by tangibles; it involves the expression of desired conditions through symbols. The automobile tail fin is trivial from an engineering standpoint but of great significance for what it symbolizes. For those concerned with planned change and the applicability of anthropology to the solution of social ills, the symbolic dimensions of slum clearance or new methods of rice cultivation must be considered in assessing the merits of planned change. It is further necessary to look at both tangible and symbolic dimensions of change from the viewpoint of those who are the "recipients" of change. The recent mass availability of automobiles in Spain has led directly to the almost unbelievable pollution of the air in Madrid, a pollution that rivals that of New York City or Los Angeles. True, the average Madrileño complains about the soot and fumes, but he very frequently tells his American friends that now Madrid is a fully developed city, just like New York or Los Angeles or Chicago. The expressions of pride may come in a choking voice, but it is pride nonetheless. The recent introduction of electricity into Taos Pueblo offends many of the ethnicity seekers (to use a local phrase) who visit it, as well as offending some of the Indians who live there. Yet it also allows the use of refrigerators and of small motors needed by Indian craftsmen to produce items for sale. Who shall decide what progress is? What is the yardstick by which we shall measure the moral and emotional parameters of a "good thing"?

I am not opposed to change, to planning, or to progress, nor am I a traditionalist who sees value in old things simply because they are old. I have raised this whole issue because it is necessary to point out that our operating mythology has raised planning for change to the level of a sacred activity wherein the primary assumptions are removed from the category of hypotheses-to-be-tested and placed into the category of truths-to-be-accepted. My point is that we cannot as students of human sociocultural systems understand the nature of change, especially planned change, unless we critically examine the assumptions that underlie and legitimate the operation of planning and the conceptualization of desirability and progress.

Man's increasing ability to control the world in which he lives is one of the most significant trends in human history. When man began to assume control over his food supply and developed controlled agricultural practices, it enabled him to devote more time to the improvement of other aspects of his culture. With increasing knowledge, changes come at a rate today that is so rapid as almost to defy belief, yet citizens of the more "developed" societies scarcely pay attention to the now routine miracles wrought by science and technology. By evolution, revolution, historical accident, or deliberately planned efforts, man has not only seen his life style change but today is actively engaged in programs deliberately intended to take even greater control of the physical and social environment in which he lives.

The participants in this symposium were asked "to examine critically some aspects of sociocultural change as *events*, as *ideologies*, and as *processes*." They were further urged to be adventurous, while at the same time it was noted: "We are obviously not going to come up with *the* definitive theory of sociocultural change, but we should be able to come up with some thoughts that will make our colleagues in the social sciences sit up and take notice, and maybe even guide them into some new directions." The invitation continued: "Humanistically oriented concern is understandable and, for most of us, desirable. But nice thoughts and wishful thinking do not necessarily make up for some hard-headed professional attempts to explain and understand change as a phenomenon. What do we know about change processes? What *can* we know? Are our theories adequate? Do we need some critical rethinking and reevaluation of anthropological contributions to the investigation and explication of change, especially planned change?"

Drawn from various subfields within anthropology, the contributors represent some of the senior members of the profession and also some of the newer and younger members. They represent a diverse background of differing philosophies, interests, and training. As anthropologists, they all have experience in researching problems related to directed culture change, and they all share a common concern over the effectiveness and morality of the changes they have observed or participated in.

Miles Richardson and Arden King take philosophical approaches to the problems of change. King argues that man, having created civilization, finds himself unable to cope with it through a failure to recognize the infinity of alternative choices of behavior open to him. Richardson warns that our neat typologies treat modernization in a sort of neo-Victorian evolutionary perspective that is not well founded. He argues that the model of Christ in which man seeks perfection is inferior to the Gilgamesh model wherein man is conscious of his mortality and potential for failure. To study man, one must use a man-sized model.

Wilfrid Bailey and Elizabeth Brandt present papers which are methodological in nature. Bailey poses the question of who shall be educated and examines the matters of what shall be taught and who shall control the processes and curricula to be used. He gives no ready answers but rather poses problems all too long overlooked in the profession. Brandt, in dealing with the role of linguistics and change, deals not only with changing language structures but also attempts to show how linguistics and social anthropology must work together if developmental change is to be understood.

Ben Wallace, James Peacock, and John Peterson present case studies, but each indicates the nature of deeper problems illustrated by their data. The intentional culture of the hippie commune and the efforts of the Muslim reformer in Indonesia illustrate the manifest and latent problems involved in attempts to restructure life styles deliberately, while the attempts at developing rural community water systems in Mississippi illustrate the unexpected changes in social relations that may come about through technological changes.

John Honigmann's paper is of special interest to anthropologists, coming as it does at a time when the profession is faced by an internal crisis over its ethical standards. Honigmann shows more faith in the integrity and ethical concern of the anthropologist than do many who clamor for rigid codes designed to curb activities deemed by them to be injurious to others in the profession and to the people we study.

As expected in this symposium, we have not come up with a definitive theory of sociocultural change; indeed we have not come up with any theory at all. We have, however, come up with a set of ideas which should stimulate and provoke those concerned with topics of change. One of my teachers once defined anthropology as a "bloodless field sport." Perhaps that statement was valid at one time, but it can no longer hold true today in the tumult of war, crisis, and extraordinary changes now in process or impending. Our so-called golden age when the lone anthropologist could "do" an entire culture is gone, never to return. Relevancy has become the magic word, as Bailey indicates in his essay, and while not neglecting our traditional province of the primitive and the simple society, we are now called upon to meet the challenges of explaining change in complex societies. The natives are increasingly restless and the anthropologists are too. People who a short time ago carried spears now use Bren guns, and scholars who debated issues of ethical neutrality in the shady groves of Academe are now working in the slum, the ghetto, the barrio, or manning the barricades in protest against social and technological innovations they abhor. It is unfortunate that William Leap's remarks as symposium discussant were not recorded. Leap in his extemporaneous remarks noted not just the restlessness of the times but also the seeming inability of anthropology to clarify its concepts to reach an understanding of this restlessness and disorder that so frequently accompany change.

We hope this symposium has added something to our understanding of change. Any general summary of the ideas expressed in these essays would be redundant. Perhaps the best statement—or is it a plea—about crisis and change is found not in the collected effort and wisdom of our contributors, but in the words of Wallace's Deva Foundation "hippies": "Us is a process of becoming fitting together & falling apart. It changes & we change & it changes. And it comes that on a warm winter day we find ourself, just sitting by the side of the barn, together people, animals, sky, trees, earth, just us . . . here. On the planet together—somehow, some way."

Gilgamesh and Christ: Two Contradictory Models of Man in Search of a Better World

MILES RICHARDSON

INTO the Temple where his mother dwelt Gilgamish[1] went, and when she saw by the look upon his face that he was bent upon going on some strange journey or upon doing some terrifying deed, his mother cried out to Shamash, The Sun God, asking him why he had given her son a heart that could never keep still. And Gilgamish, hearing her cry, said to her, "Peace O woman! I am Gilgamish, and it must be that I shall see everything, learn everything, understand everything." Then his mother said to him, "These longings are yours, O Gilgamish, because not all of you is mortal. Two thirds of your flesh is as the flesh of Gods and only one third is as the flesh of men. And because of the Gods' flesh that is on you, you must be always daring, always restless. But yet, O my son, you have not immortal life. You must die because part of you is man. Yea, Gilgamish, even you must die, and go down into the House of Dust."

And Gilgamish, hearing his mother say this, groaned loudly, terribly; and tears flowed down his cheeks; no word that was said to him might content him. He groaned, he wept, even although in the court of the Temple he heard the women sing:

"Who is splendid among men,
Who is glorious among heroes?"

And answer back, one to the other:

"Gilgamish is splendid among men
Gilgamish is glorious among heroes."

In a while he rose up and said, "O Ninsunna, O my mother, what is it to die?"

Then Ninsunna, his mother, made answer, and said, "It is

7

to go into the abode out of which none ever returns; it is to go
into the dark abyss of the dread Goddess, Irkalla. They who
dwell there are without light; the beings that are there eat of
the dust and feed on the mud."

So his mother said, and Gilgamish, the great king, groaned
aloud, and tears flowed down his face. (Colum 1930: 19-20)

[*Time moves; the scene changes.*]

And when they had crucified him, they divided his garments
among them by casting lots; then they sat down and kept watch
over him there. And over his head they put the charge against
him, which read, "This is Jesus the King of the Jews." Then two
robbers were crucified with him, one on the right and one on
the left. And those who passed by derided him, wagging their
heads and saying, "You who would destroy the temple and build
it in three days, save yourself! If you are the Son of God, come
down from the cross." So also the chief priests, with the scribes
and elders, mocked him, saying, "He saved others; he cannot save
himself. He is the King of Israel; let him come down now from
the cross, and we will believe in him. He trusts in God; let God
deliver him now, if he desires him; for he said, I am the Son of
God." And the robbers who were crucified with him also reviled
him in the same way.

Now from the sixth hour there was darkness over all the
land until the ninth hour. And about the ninth hour Jesus cried
with a loud voice . . . "My God, my God, why hast thou forsaken me?" (Matthew 27:35-46)

Perhaps since the time of the australopithecines—those tiny brained,
large jawed creatures who walked bipedally across Africa at the
beginning of Pleistocene—change in the human species has been a
series of adaptations to being human. For instance, the increase in
brain size from the australopithecines to Neanderthal man reflects
an adaptation to the human mode of exploiting the environment
(Brace and Montagu 1965). The development of a self, which
emerged through man's ability to treat himself as an object, is still
another example (Hallowell 1959, 1968). In large measure, adaptation to being human is adjustment to the ability to symbolize, the
ability to envisage a future, immediate or distant, and to organize
one's energies, experiences, and desires in terms of that future. It
is the ability to create a future and then to act as if that future
were real and achievable.

Nowhere is this human ability so marked as in the case of death.
Apparently man is the only life form that can terrify itself with

visions of its own extinction. Once man has terrified himself with his visions, he struggles to overcome them, and the ultimate criterion of any utopia worthy of the name is a world without death.

The figures of Gilgamesh and Christ offer two contradictory models of man confronting his own knowledge. Both figures try to solve the problem of death; they both seek eternal life. Gilgamesh fails; Christ succeeds. Yet it is in Gilgamesh's failure rather than in Christ's success that we get a glimpse of the human condition and an example of our task as anthropologists.

Gilgamesh is the central figure in an epic that dates back to approximately 2,000 B.C.[2] In the epic Gilgamesh is king over the city state of Uruk. Even for those days, Gilgamesh is an extraordinary king. He is restless, strong, and full of lust, "leaving no virgin to her lover, neither the warrior's daughter nor the wife of the noble." He is two-thirds God and one-third man, and none can withstand him.

The people of Uruk begin to mutter among themselves about Gilgamesh and turn to the gods for relief from his restlessness. In answer the gods make Gilgamesh's equal, Enkidu, and send him to live in the wilderness with the animals. Enkidu loses his innocence to a temple harlot and from her hears about Gilgamesh. He brags to to the harlot that he will go to Uruk and challenge Gilgamesh.

When he enters the city, he will cry out, "I am the strongest here, I have come to change the old order, I am he who was born in the hills, I am he who is the strongest of all."

Enkidu leaves for Uruk. As he approaches, people compare him with Gilgamesh: "He is the spit of Gilgamesh. He is shorter. He is bigger of bone. Now Gilgamesh has met his match." Gilgamesh walks out in the street. Enkidu blocks his way. "They grappled, holding each other like bulls. They broke the doorposts and the wall shook, they snorted like bulls locked together." Gilgamesh throws Enkidu, and Enkidu immediately recognizes Gilgamesh's superiority. They embrace and become fast friends.

Gilgamesh and Enkidu set out for the Land of the Cedars, for Gilgamesh wants to write his name in that place where no man has been. Enkidu warns him of the monster, Humbaba, who watches over the land. Gilgamesh with scorn replies, "Where is the man who can clamber to heaven? Only the gods live forever with glorious Shamash, but as for us men, our days are numbered, our occupations are a breath of wind. How is this, already you are afraid! I will go first although I am your lord, and you may safely call out, 'Forward, there is nothing to fear.'" With Enkidu shamed into following him,

Gilgamesh enters the Land of Cedars. They encounter Humbaba, and after a furious struggle the two friends succeed in killing him.

When they return, the goddess Ishtar sees them and is overwhelmed by Gilgamesh's beauty. She offers him her love, but Gilgamesh reminds her of how she has treated her former lovers: how she lured the lion into a trap; how she tricked the stallion into being captured and broken to the bit; and how she turned the shepherd into a wolf, so that "now his own herd-boys chase him away, his own hounds worry his flank." Gilgamesh suggests that the same thing may happen to him.

Ishtar is furious. She rushes off to her father and complains, "My father, Gilgamesh has heaped insults on me; he has told over all my abominable behaviour, all my tainted acts." Her father says that she has brought it upon herself and that he will not listen to her. But she threatens to break open the door of hell and let all the dead out. So her father changes his mind and makes for her a bull of heaven. She turns the bull loose on earth, and

> with his first snort he slew a hundred men, and again he slew two hundred, he slew three hundred; with his second snort hundreds more fell dead. With his third snort he charged Enkidu, but he dodged aside and leapt upon the Bull and seized it by the horns. The Bull of Heaven foamed in his face, it brushed him with the thick of his tail. Endiku cried to Gilgamesh, "My friend, we boasted that we would leave enduring names behind us. Now thrust in your sword between the nape and the horns." So Gilgamesh followed the Bull, he seized the thick of its tail, he thrust the sword between the nape and the horns and slew the Bull.

Ishtar looked down at them and uttered a curse: "Woe to Gilgamesh, for he has scorned me in killing the Bull of Heaven." When Enkidu heard these words he tore out the Bull's right thigh and tossed it in her face saying, "If I could lay my hands on you, it is this I should do to you, and lash the entrails on your side."

Shortly afterwards, Enkidu has a number of dreams, each about his own death. He tells Gilgamesh,

> Last night I dreamed again, my friend. The heavens moaned and the earth replied; I stood alone before an awful being; his face was sombre like the black bird of the storm. He fell upon me with the talons of an eagle and he held me fast, pinioned with his claws, till I smothered; then he transformed me so that my arms became wings covered with feathers. He turned his stare towards me, and led me away to the palace of Irkalla, the Queen of Darkness, to the house from which none who enters ever returns,

down the road from which there is no coming back. There is the house whose people sit in darkness; dust is their food and clay their meat. They are clothed like birds with wings for covering, they see no light, they sit in darkness.

Enkidu becomes very ill and after twelve days of suffering he dies on the twelfth night. At the first light of dawn, Gilgamesh calls together the counselors of Uruk and cries out:

Hear me, great ones of Uruk,
I weep for Enkidu, my friend,
Bitterly moaning like a woman mourning
I weep for my brother.
O Enkidu, the wild ass and the gazelle
That were father and mother,
All four-footed creatures who fed with you
Weep for you,
. . . . .
The mountain we climbed where we slew the watchman
Weeps for you,
Ula of Elam and dear Euphrates
Where once we drew water for the waterskins,
The warriors of strong-walled Uruk
Where the Bull of Heaven was killed,
Weep for you.
. . . . .
The tillers and harvesters
Who brought grain for you once
Mourn for you now.
The servants who anointed your body
Mourn for you now;
The harlot who anointed you with fragrant oil
Laments for you now.
The women of the palace, who brought you a wife
With the ring of your choice,
Lament for you now.
O my young brother Enkidu, my dearest friend,
What is this sleep which holds you now?
You are lost in the dark and cannot hear me.

The death of Enkidu awakens the fear in Gilgamesh that he too may well die. "Bitterly Gilgamesh wept for his friend Enkidu; he wandered over the wilderness as a hunter, he roamed over the plains; in bitterness he cried, 'How can I rest, how can I be at peace? Despair is in my heart.' "

Driven by his fear, Gilgamesh travels to find the one human

who does have immortal life, Utnapishtim, the Faraway. In his journey, Gilgamesh encounters one difficulty after another. Some of these wear away at his great strength; others, such as the woman of the vine, try to confuse his purpose. She asks, "Gilgamesh, where are you hurrying to? You will never find that life for which you are looking. So fill your belly with good things; day and night, night and day, dance and be merry, feast and rejoice. Let your clothes be fresh, bathe yourself in water, cherish the little child that holds your hand, and make your wife happy in your embrace; for this too is the lot of man." But Gilgamesh's fear, fear of a man who is two-thirds god, will not let him rest nor rejoice.

Gilgamesh crosses the waters of death, and as he nears the shore, Utnapishtim sees him and wonders who is this poor traveler who staggers toward him. Aloud, he asks, "What is your name, you who come here wearing the skins of beasts, with your cheeks starved and your face drawn? Where are you hurrying to now?"

Gilgamesh explains that he is looking for life without death. Utnapishtim snorts, "There is no permanence. Do we build a house to stand for ever, do we seal a contract to hold for all time?" Gilgamesh replies, "How was it that you came to enter the company of the gods and to possess everlasting life?" Utnapishtim then tells him the story of the flood.

Once there was no death. Men did not die. Because they did not die, they became numerous. As men increased in numbers, they began making more and more noise. The noise that they made became so great that the gods complained that they could no longer sleep properly. So the gods decided to wash the world clean of men, and they let loose a deluge. However, one god had a human friend, Utnapishtim, and he told his friend to build a boat because the world was to be flooded. Utnapishtim listened to his god and built a boat big enough to contain all of his gold, his family and kin, the beasts of the field, and his craftsmen. The rains covered the earth, and only those in the boat did not drown. When the waters subsided, Utnapishtim prepared a sacrifice. When the gods smelled it, "they gathered like flies over the sacrifice." Satiated with the sacrifice and feeling remorseful over flooding the world, the gods granted Utnapishtim immortal life.

When Utnapishtim is finished with the story, he says to Gilgamesh, "As for you, Gilgamesh, who will assemble the gods for your sake, so that you may find that life for which you are searching?"

But Utnapishtim relents and puts Gilgamesh to a test. If Gilgamesh can stay awake for six days and seven nights, Utnapishtim will help him. No sooner than the test begins, Gilgamesh falls asleep. Utnapishtim remarks with scorn, "Look at him now, the strong man who would have everlasting life, even now the mists of sleep are drifting over him."

Utnapishtim lets Gilgamesh sleep for seven nights and then awakens him. When Gilgamesh realizes what he has done, he asks in despair, "What shall I do, O Utnapishtim, where shall I go? Already the thief in the night has hold of my limbs, death inhabits my room; wherever my foot rests, there I find death."

Wearily, Gilgamesh turns to go, but Utnapishtim tells him of one more chance to gain eternal life. At the bottom of the waters of death is a plant which restores lost youth to man. Gilgamesh goes to the bottom of the ocean and succeeds in getting the plant. In the company of Urshanabi, the ferryman, he crosses the waters of death and makes for Uruk. The two stop to rest beside a well of cool water. While Gilgamesh is preoccupied, a snake comes from the bottom of the well and eats the plant. Gilgamesh sits down and weeps, "O Urshanabi, was it for this that I toiled with my hands, is it for this I have wrung out my heart's blood? For myself I have gained nothing; not I, but the beast of the earth has joy of it now. I found a sign and now I have lost it. Let us leave the boat on the bank and go."

On the outskirts of Uruk, Gilgamesh looks at his city and says to Urshanabi, "Climb up on the wall of Uruk, inspect its foundation terrace, and examine well the brickwork; see if it is not of burnt bricks; and did not the seven wise men lay these foundations? One third of the whole is city, one third is garden, and one third is field, with the precinct of the goddess Ishtar. These parts and the precinct are all Uruk."

This too was the work of Gilgamesh, the king, who knew the countries of the world. "He was wise, he saw mysteries and knew secret things, he brought us a tale of the days before the flood. He went on a long journey, was weary, worn out with labour, and returning engraved on a stone the whole story."

The epic of Gilgamesh is the account of a man who wants to see everything, learn everything, and understand everything. He has these desires to an extraordinary degree because he is two-thirds God. He feels the approach of death more than the ordinary man, and he strives to conquer it. Yet he fails. He fails because he is one-third man. As his godly part drives Gilgamesh to risk great achievements, so his human part insures that he will fail. He is a tragic hero, a person magnificent in strength, splendid in appearance, courageous in heart, but with one fatal fault: he is one-third man. His epic is an account of what constitutes man's lot. Man's lot is that he question, but it is equally man's lot that he receive no answer.

The figure of Christ provides a very different model of man in search of a better world. There are, of course, several Christs. There is the Christ of Spanish America who teaches man how to suffer (Richardson, Bode, and Pardo 1971); there is King Jesus who rides his white horse ahead of the black congregations of the South; and then there is the swingingest figure of them all—Jesus Christ: Superstar.

The figure that I am referring to is the Protestant Christ, especially the traditional, orthodox one. This is the Christ who is somehow both an effeminate figure who bids you in a sweet voice to turn the other cheek and a merciless individual who will watch you burn in Hell—and not bat an eyelash. In any attribute, he is perfection, unalterable perfection. If there are any of his movements, desires, or expressions that you do not understand, it is because of your inability to comprehend, because of your limitations as a mere human. Thus, when Jesus said on the cross, "My God, my God, why hast thou forsaken me?" he may have been posing a puzzle for mankind, but he most certainly was not expressing doubt about his own godhood.

This traditional Christ has the same task as Gilgamesh: to conquer death. Yet in every other respect he is in complete contrast to Gilgamesh. Unlike Gilgamesh, Christ is fully God. To be sure, he has a human exterior, and he has to suffer the pain and indignities that this human exterior brings him. But within, he is pure God—and he knows it. In contrast to Gilgamesh's aristocracy, Christ on earth belongs to the lower class. While Gilgamesh performs great feats of physical prowess, Jesus works miracles of healing and raising the dead. Only when he chases the money changers out of the temple does Jesus exhibit a physical strength. He is almost sexless and is free of lust; Gilgamesh, on the other hand, leaves "no virgin to her lover."

Gilgamesh responds with great feeling only to his close friend, Enkidu. He has no message for other men; what he seeks, he seeks for himself. He seeks what only the gods have: eternal life. Driven by the hope that he will not fail, Gilgamesh risks all in the effort. With success literally in his hand, he is careless for a brief moment and fails. Jesus, on the other hand, is sensitive to the conditions and feelings of all people, even strangers. He is a teacher with a message. He teaches that if people will follow him and believe in him, they will have eternal life. To demonstrate that he is God, he does the one thing that only God can do: he conquers death. Knowing that he cannot fail, Jesus allows himself to be crucified. He is reborn after three days, and in doing so, he shows all that he is God. All those who believe in him will likewise be reborn.

The model that the image of Christ provides is a model of progress, success, utopia. It is the picture of man as God. If man has sufficient faith in God, he can conquer any obstacle, even death. If man will but submit himself to the right authority, if he will but follow the right creed, then he will succeed. He can remake the world. Man can achieve perfection—if not now, then in the next five minutes; if not then, a year from now, a century, two centuries, a thousand years from now. The millennium will come. The perfect world, a world without sin, without oppression, without racial hatred, without atomic fallout, without pollution, without all those actions and emotions that make man less than God, is attainable. Man can aspire to be God.

Such an aspiration, of course, is not limited to Christians. As Peacock and Kirsch (1970:202-217) have pointed out, the Christ model has become secularized into a basic tenet of American culture. Working with a model which calls for man to remake his evil world into the shape of God's saintly one, secular American culture has produced a model of two contrasting types. One type is a constellation of all the undesirable characteristics; the second type is the epitome of all that is good, true, and useful. Despite occasional minor reverses, movement is from the first, the bad, to the second, the good.

Such polar contrasts appear frequently in the scholarly discussions about modernization-developmental processes into a type of evolutionism that is as ethnocentric as the most brash Victorian theoretical scheme (Hoetink 1965). The scholar proceeds by contrasting type one, traditional society, with type two, modern society. Societies become modernized and developed to the extent that they leave type one and approach type two. So far so good. But the traditional type is often a patchwork construct pieced together with features of the most backward societies. The traditional type is Papa Doc's Haiti in Hell. The modern type is a glittering edifice elegantly devised from the best features of the most advanced societies. The modern type is General Ike's America in Heaven.

In a recent seminar on Latin American agricultural development, the speaker was contrasting the agricultural practices of type one, the Nicaraguan peasant, with type two, the American agro-businessman. To make his point, the speaker showed a slide of the peasant striding alongside his oxen as they pulled a solid wooden-wheeled cart across the Nicaraguan landscape. The speaker asked us to compare the cart with automated mechanical creatures that waddle their way through the California lettuce fields. In his accompanying remarks the speaker showed no appreciation of the antiquity of the cart or of its effectiveness in uneven terrain. He ignored the ingenuity of the peasant in utilizing scarce resources, nor did he mention the asymmetrical power relations between Nicaragua and the United States, relations that may have helped create the limited, scarce environment in which the Nicaraguan works.

The employment of the model of contrasting types is not restricted to agricultural studies. The management field utilizes the model when it compares the practices of management in traditional society with those of modern society. One student of management contrasts the Mexican and North American organization men in this fashion: "Fear" characterizes the relationship between the typical Mexican manager and his superiors. He attempts to "avoid" or "outmaneuver" his organizational equals. He sees subordinates as "unreliable and untrustworthy tools." In contrast, the typical United States type "respects" his superiors, "cooperates" with his equals, and sees his subordinates as "helpers" (Fayerweather 1959:31-41; Richardson 1966).

In political science the employment of the model of two contrasting types makes the Latin American system of elite replacement equal to political instability and immaturity, unrepresentative government, and apathetic masses. It makes the system that the United States uses to replace its elite equal to political stability and maturity, democratic government, and a participating, involved citizenry. These equations justly earn Leeds's contempt as being "pernicious in their ethnocentricism [and in] their evangelical assurance of righteousness" (1968:85).

Evangelical arrogance is by no means restricted to political science. One can detect it, now and again, among the voices raised in the not so deliberate meetings of the American Anthropological Association. In that nervous body, it passes as very radical chic, expounded by bourgeois adventurers and adventuresses, their minds bedazzled by the image of themselves as Christ—Che Guevara incarnate leading the admiring masses to victory against the capitalistic, imperialistic, warmongers of Wall Street.

The Christ model of man in search of a better world is at its best when it is used as a model for action. Any model which guarantees that whosoever follows it will live forever (and succeed always) is going to be popular. However forceful the model may be in stimulating action, as a model for comprehension it produces farcical results. For it is a model that lacks tolerance, humor, and skepticism, that lacks an appreciation of alternatives, that lacks all those attributes that characterize the anthropological perspective.

Instead of depicting man as God, the Gilgamesh model pictures man as hero. Instead of being a model of utopia, it is a model of effort, of drive, of risk, and of failure. Gilgamesh strives to be perfect, but he is man and he fails. In these two acts of effort and of collapse, we find ourselves.

We utilize the magic of symbols, of culture, to construct an image of the future. With our magic, we reify that image and convince ourselves and others that the image is not an image but reality itself. With the pure commitment of the insane, we proceed toward that tantalizing image, full of confidence that we will succeed.

The future that we seek may be immediate or distant, it may evoke the behavior of a few or stimulate action on the part of many. It may be the modest image of two anthropologists at the bar discussing Lévi-Strauss over bourbon and branch, or it may be the hopeful vision of a nation meeting its obligation to its poor. But the future in the image is imaginary; it is our fantasy of what we expect to encounter, and not what we will actually meet. Even our best images, our most scientific models, our most elegant ethnosemantic charts have this flaw. Because we as men live within a world that is symbolic and not real, we err, inevitably so. Sooner or later our symbols depart too far from reality and we crash against the unexpected. Instead of discussing Lévi-Strauss, the two anthropologists get drunk (which may be an improvement); instead of offering dignity to its poor, the nation casts them out. The very thing that leads us on insures that we will fail. It is because of the ability to utilize symbols that we strive; it is because of the same ability that we fail.

Although we fail, we cannot rest with failure. That which makes us human picks us up from the floor and we are off, as Utnapishtim might say, on another fool's errand. Only when we cease being human will we cease failing, and only when we cease failing will we cease striving to accomplish what cannot be accomplished. Yes, we may be fools, but we are heroic fools. We will end the world not with a whimper, but with a big, loud bang.

If this is the way man is, then cannot he, like Gilgamesh, take satisfaction in what he can accomplish and in what he is? If he cannot achieve perfection, he can nonetheless build what no other animal can build, and if he cannot be God, he can be what he is. What man is, is what he is now—and what he was at the beginning of the Pleistocene. He is a two-legged primate, struggling. He is "always daring, always restless, with a heart that can never keep still"; he is "bent upon going on some strange journey or upon doing some terrifying deed."

To recite the epic of man is the task of the anthropologist. He has the unique charge of celebrating man's acts. He is man's poet. As man's poet, the anthropologist tells of how man plays his part in a drama that is simultaneously one of horror and one of hope. He has to tell of Auschwitz where man bathed his own kind in poison gas. He has to tell of My Lai and to recite to the rhythm of his own guilt the words of our time: "Waste them." The anthropologist must speak of man's failures, for these are the things that men do. But when he is weary of man's defeats, he can sing of other occasions when man somehow reaches out to other men and expresses with a few words the hopes of all. Such an occasion took place when a Southern black man stood in Washington, D.C., and shook the world with "I have a dream." Still another occasion took place when after a long, bitter war Chief Joseph of the Nez Perce Indians spoke for us:

I am tired of fighting. Our chiefs are killed. Looking Glass is dead. Toohulhulsote is dead. The old men are all dead. It is the young men who say no and yes. He who led the young men is dead. It is cold and we have no blankets. The little children are freezing to death. My people, some of them, have run away to the hills and have no blankets, no food. No one knows where they are—perhaps they are freezing to death.

I want to have time to look for my children and see how many of them I can find. Maybe I shall find them among the dead. Hear me my chiefs, I am tired. My heart is sad and sick. From where the sun now stands, I will fight no more forever.

Anthropology has the unique charge of celebrating the whole of mankind, but it has a special obligation to those groups who have little power, who live at minimal subsistence levels; whom the currents of history have bypassed, whom the superpowers ignore or manipulate to their own advantage. Paul Radin wrote in 1933 that it is to these people that the anthropologist owes his first loyalty (1933:x). Surely by now we are aware of this obligation. Likewise we are by now aware of the delicate nature of this relationship. The fine strands of the relationship between the anthropologist and these groups cannot support the heavy sentiment of the romantic anthropologist leading "his people" on to victory, just as they cannot withstand the scientific arrogance of those who look for subjects and not for informants.

Yet anthropology is anthropology. It is not the study of men, but of man. To contemplate man we cannot use a model based on the smooth flow of action produced by the uneventful life of a god, but rather we need a model based on the outrageous contradiction of an imperfect man seeking perfection. The god model of Christ leads us away from the study of man because it bedazzles us with the promise that someday we will cease to be human and become God. The man model of Gilgamesh holds out no such hope. With it we can come closer to understanding what it is to be human. With it we can tell the story of man. In the future, in the distant future, perhaps some will find the epic that we have written and read there that man knew the countries of the world. "He was wise, he saw mysteries and knew secret things, he brought us a tale of the days before the flood. He went on a long journey, was weary, worn out with labour, and returning engraved on a stone the whole story."

NOTES

1. The English spelling of Gilgamesh varies, with Gilgamesh being most common. Colum spells the name Gilgamish.
2. This summary and the quotations contained within it are from Sandars (1960). Sandars has done an excellent job of combining scholarship with a highly readable text, and the reader is referred to this source for additional background material on Gilgamesh and his times.

REFERENCES

Brace, C. Loring, and M. F. Ashley Montagu, 1965. *Man's Evolution* (New York: Macmillan).
Colum, Padraic, 1930. *Orpheus: Myths of the World* (New York: Macmillan).
Fayerweather, J., 1959. *The Executive Overseas* (Syracuse, N.Y.: Syracuse University Press).
Hallowell, A. Irving, 1959. Behavioral Evolution and the Emergence of the Self. In *Evolution and Anthropology: A Centennial Appraisal,* Betty J. Meggers, ed. (Washington, D.C.: Anthropological Society of Washington).
———, 1968. Self, Society and Culture in Phylogenetic Perspective. In *Culture: Man's Adaptive Dimension,* M. F. Ashley Montagu, ed. (London: Oxford University Press).
Hoetink, H. 1965. El nuevo evolucionismo. *América Latina* 8:26-42.
Leeds, Anthony, 1968. Comment on Political Instability in Latin America: The Cross-Cultural Test of a Causal Model. *Latin American Research Review* 3:79-86.
Peacock, James L., and A. Thomas Kirsch, 1970. *The Human Direction* (New York: Appleton-Century-Crofts).
Radin, Paul, 1933. *Method and Theory in Ethnology* (New York: McGraw-Hill).
Richardson, Miles, 1966. The Possibility of an Anthropology-Management Symbiosis. *South Eastern Latin Americanist* 10:1-3.
———, Barbara Bode, and Marta Eugenia Pardo, 1971. The Image of Christ in Spanish America as a Model for Suffering: An Exploratory Note. *Journal of Inter-American Studies* 13:246-257.
Sandars, N. K., 1960. *The Epic of Gilgamesh* (London: Penguin Books).

The Five-Thousand-Year Challenge

ARDEN R. KING

ANY anthropological approach to development and directed culture change must of necessity be focused on present and future human behavior. Such an obvious statement, however, has implications for a problem basic to both ends of the development axis: the challenge of civilizational culture. It is my contention that man has been unable to develop a mode of planning, a definition of goals, and a conscious rationality commensurate with the complexity that is civilization. For at least five thousand years man in civilization has answered its challenge in ways appropriate to family and kin, to the tribal camp, to the village, and—at the very best—to complex peasant levels. Further, man's efforts to understand and direct the course of culture change in civilization have been fated to disappointment and disaster by reason of incorrect analogy and attempted homology to past culture experience. The understanding of civilizational culture lies not in the use of simpler cultural patterns as models, nor in its definition as qualitatively different through substantive accumulation of culture. It is here proposed that the salient characteristic of civilization is the cognitively recognized infinity of choice for *possible* behavior presented to man. By the phrase "cognitively recognized infinity of choice" I am, among other things, referring to the presence and development of conscious and rational knowledge systems through written records, their dissemination through formally organized educational systems, and the increase in the efficiency and frequency of communication of the knowledge of the variety of cultural behavior used by man. As men we have refused this infinity of choice. Herein lies the crux of difficulties inherent in development programs and in directed culture change. For the source of development is civilizational culture, but developers have not utilized civilization as models for development and change. Developers, as men of civilization, present noncivilizational models to developing countries, but the vehicle of presentation is civilization. Let us now consider these propositions in some detail.

The difference between development and directed culture change on the one hand and culture change as a process on the other presents difficulties of delineation. Culture change has usually been conceived by anthropologists as a relatively noncognitive process, and over the long range of culture history this seems true. Nevertheless, any conscious, rational planning for future events, or in the face of disaster, or in the solution of pressing problems, constitutes something closely akin to development and directed culture change as we view it in the late twentieth century. In this sense then we have development in all cultures, but development and directed culture change are more characteristics of civilization than other cultural forms. The variety of learned, unshared behavior in the total society brings this about by placing great value on more continuous rational and conscious planning of human activity. The potential disruptions originating in those intracultural differences found in civilization apparently can only be overridden in this fashion. Here development and directed culture change are differentiated from culture change as a general process.

As a conscious process, development and directed culture change rest on the assumption by both the developer and those being developed that all such change emphasizes modernity, hence civilization, as a desirable end. However, we have postulated that the developers of civilization share with all civilized men the inability to comprehend fully their culture in a rational, logical, conscious manner that is applicable to civilization exclusively. Development as a process creates a situation in which this is startlingly apparent. The knowledge of human behavioral variety confronts the developer by extending his range of cross-cultural knowledge. Those being developed encounter the complexity that is civilization. But the form of conscious and rational planning for development contains within it the assumption that our modes of accommodation to civilization are not in its own terms but in terms of family, kin, village, and neighborhood. Consider, for example, assumptions that a particular form of mother-child relationship is universal, that in all cities, new or modernizing old ones, something like a neighborhood should be sought—in sum, that primary group affiliations derived from past models are necessary to all human societies. "Civilized" man is an occupant rather than a practitioner of civilization. Consequently, as developer he presents the modern world in terms of the values and priorities of a villager. And this to villagers! Civilization is not village life, and only those village practices historically antecedent to the particular civilization have any hope of ready function. In this sense then, unless the developer can bring himself to be civilized man, development to the state of civilization will always be an incomplete process.

Although of considerable significance to the practitioners of development, nonsocial science definitions and usages of the concept of civilization are beyond the confines of this paper. Social scientists generally have conceived of civilization as a form of culture. Some have seen the concepts as interchangeable, others have differentiated civilization as a more complex and substantively greater form of culture. A few have designated "civilization" as qualitatively different from "other cultures." Although Tylor at times used "culture" and "civilization" interchangeably, he viewed cultural evolution as ending with a qualitatively different form he termed civilization. Most anthropologists in the attempt to avoid ethnocentric judgments have turned to measurements sometimes characterized as norms of internal efficiency such as writing, technology, and science. To these, scholars such as V. G. Childe added the presence of cities, population heterogeneity linked with a complex division of labor, and rationalized concentrations of political and economic power. Some notable scholars have proposed definitions based on the moral order. Redfield is a case in point: "the moral order, though shaken by civilization, is also, in civilization taken by reason into charge. . . . The moral order in early civilization is taken into charge by specialists as a philosophical problem" (1953:119-120). For anthropologists, two main factors seem to characterize civilization: vastly increased complexity and different levels of integration. Another way of saying it is that there has been a significant intensification of the individuation of events and persons in substance and time. By this I have in mind the increase in the detail of record keeping concerning events and individuals and their part in them. Events and the individuals involved have become increasingly discrete, which marks an important process of the history of civilization. The usual way to characterize this process is to point to such phenomena as dogma and organized religion, philosophical systems, nationalism intensified by language and geographical area, and so on. These are functionally over-arching concepts which serve to bind the varied units that constitute a civilization. Attempts to differentiate early civilizations from those of the present day usually do not deal with the levels of integration sought after but with the complexities of content and the means of making these available to the societies concerned.

For the past five thousand years we have refused the challenge of the complex culture content accompanying civilization. We have attempted the accommodation of the possibility of infinite experience and knowledge through the retrogressive referral of demands for their organization and a higher level of integration to models of earlier cant. There is a regression to nonverbal levels of unity, integration, and nonconscious valuing of experience. I have specific reference here to those modes of behavior shared with other mammals and primates which are learned by all men through nonlinguistic communication. These have been acquired early in socialization and thus lie deeply imbedded in shared personality structure. I shall return to this in a more detailed fashion later. In addition, this regression to nonverbal levels is not only characteristic of man as a whole, but it is also frighteningly expressive of the sources of social science models. So it is, then, that social scientists and developers have drawn their models from those aspects of tribal and village life and culture that have acquired their emotional surcharge of value via nonverbal communication. It is in these and the conceptual valuing of family and kin (even though consciously moribund) that we derive our absolutely held standards of what it is to be human. I suggest that social science is so predictively inept because it has addressed itself to the wrong phenomenon. We hold as ideals to be sought not the civilizational culture we use nor the civilizational culture we propose in development, but those which served an earlier day.

If man has not coped with civilization now or in the past, to what levels of behavior may we turn in order to understand what we do cope with? I suspect that a significant part of such an explication lies in the traditions of learned behavior we share with other life forms. Although we cannot here discuss all the relevant facts from ethology, there are insights to be gained by juxtaposing some of its findings and the presumed incapacity of man to cope with civilization.

We must extend our understanding of traditions of learned behavior in terms of both evolution and continuity. As Earl Count has implied in his insightful writing, we are now more clearly able to distinguish instinct, universal aspects of behavior, and learned behaviors. Count's distinction between programmed potential for behavior and programmed behavior is critical (Count 1958-1959, 1968, 1969). The importance of this distinction is indicated when we realize how little we know concerning the behavioral potential possessed by any life form. What seems to be emerging from ethological investigations is that we must all learn to be vertebrates, to be mammals, to be primates, to be human.

It is then pertinent to ask whether much of that which has been defined as instinctual behavior, as genetically instigated and determined behavior, is a misidentification of the long tradition of learned vertebrate, or mammalian, or primate behavior. Humans share with other forms of our taxonomic ilk the ways of learning to behave, and in behaving we cement our relationship to them.

How then do we differentiate between humans and nonhumans? Certainly the potential for behavior is different, but we have not lost the potential to learn to behave as vertebrates, or mammals, or primates. In such circumstances more finely drawn lines of distinction between the behavior of life forms emerge: the data are more narrowly derived from phenomenological circumstance. The preciseness and arbitrariness of linguistic communication evoke the standard whereby human behavior can be distinguished from that of our behavioral ancestors and co-freres and, through this the elaboration of behavior in its conscious, rational, and logical modes, move us toward a more precise delineation of behavior. Where we share modes of behavior with other vertebrates, mammals, and primates, we employ other means of communication, hence the lack of preciseness and a commitment to more limited yet more diffuse states of being.

But there is more than this which is shared between these life forms. Individual organisms as the source of new behavior continuously display a vague recognition that the potential for behavior is only partly utilized. In consequence there is some apprehension of other possible behavior. This need not necessarily lie within the potential of actualized behavior but simply in the adumbration of behavior beyond the potential. In the context of behavioral evolution both of these possibilities imply that a keening for future lost is necessarily a requisite for such evolution. A tradition of learned behavior for unachieved but dimly perceived behavior could be the condition of selection for evolution. Behavior that is sought for but unattainable can easily be part of learning, and it can thereby be actualized once the potential is available. But such a state of affairs is also the source of disruptive social behavior and in this sense is related to our seeming inability to cope with civilization and through this to the inconsistencies of development programs.

The implication of the foregoing is that behavioral evolution has led to the increasing individuation of behavior. And, further, that cultural evolution leads to the rise of civilization which in turn is most easily characterized in a processual sense as the increasing discreteness of events. The increasing individuation of personality, personal acts, and social acts then all stand in contrast to the retention of the learned tradition of behavior we share with other life forms. We have asserted that these learned traditions of behavior emphasize modes of communication other than linguistic. It is here that we need to recognize another process that is implicit in parts of the foregoing argument, namely, part and parcel of the successful survival of any life form is the contextual meaning of its whole of experience. The unexpected arising from the utilization of unexploited potential or the seeking beyond potential somehow must be kept within the range of coping. The means by which man achieves this is through shared behavior learned in the early years of life history through nonlinguistic communication, although linguistic communication obviously becomes more important as time passes. I suspect that much of what we learn in this manner are the vertebrate, mammalian, and primate traditions. That is, only after we have acquired the bases of our identity, personally and socially, does the uniquely human mode of intensifying the individuation of events come fully into play. By that time we have established the means whereby the world is valued, even though we may attempt to transmute them by assigning linguistic modes to them. The demands of civilization are in counterposition to those of the social groups by means of which we achieve the meaning of the totality of experience. With the intensification of individuation coincident with the development of civilization, the individual can no longer cope with nor fulfill the demands placed upon him. We then deny civilization because we do not have the means at hand for our individual realization of it.

Does the denial of civilization mean that it is not human because kin and neighborhood cannot be applied to its challenge? Are we behaviorally equipped only to create civilization but not to cope with it? Is civilization an example of the keening for future lost in that we always apprehend more than we learn or achieve? And is what we learn to apprehend never fulfilled? I cannot give answers to these questions. All we can observe is that we reject the implications of civilization and in so doing we find ourselves unable to cope with civilization as a whole. Does our rejection of civilization represent a universal inability to cope with it? The fact that I am most uncertain of our ability to cope derives from my suspicion that vertebrate, mammalian, and primate learned behaviors establish the bases of human individual personality and society. Our inability to make the totality of civilization meaningful, to utilize civilization, seems to indicate that man's behavior is not equal to the potential of cultural behavior.

Nevertheless, for me the significant quality of behavioral evolution has been the ability of the organism to find ways and means of coping with the constant apprehension of new experience, of acquiring new behavior, and of coming up with a holistic statement sufficient to a succeeding evolutionary stage. Given the whole of human experience, can we expect that civilization will demand any less in terms of holism? Or does civilization decrease the possibility that it can be achieved? The relating of the individual personality to the totality of civilizational culture, however, has never been in terms of its most salient characteristic, namely, that civilization is potentially a culture of infinite choice of behaviors. Although we obviously attempt to avoid it by designating limiting qualities, boundaries, and the like, the cognitive realization of infinity is more a feature of man in civilized culture than in other forms. But in some important sense, the nearer such realization approaches cognition the more effort is spent avoiding it. This points up the continuous adumbration of infinity evoked by man's experience with civilization.

If we then characterize the appearance of civilization as the entrance into the realm of infinite possibility for man, then how do we explain his refusal to deal with it? There is a suppression of infinite possibility by emphasizing those aspects of culture in which the nonverbal means of communication are as important as symbolic ones. The achievement of group unity through the holistic definition of man and the universe is not achieved through civilizational means. If the means of coping with civilization are not civilizational, then how can its demands be met?

Let us look at the situation once more. We have postulated the persistence of learned traditions of behavior through the course of behavioral evolution to man. We have also postulated the lack of full development of potential in any life form and, deriving from this, the possibility of discovering new behavior in each life form either through the utilization of this potential for behavior not in the learned tradition of that animal or in the striving for behavior felt but not achievable. We have also intimated that the acquisition of a tradition of behavior also provides, despite its partial use of potential, the means for coping with the totality of behavior by defining its meaning. In all the traditions of learned behavior, nonverbal means of communicating this behavior are exclusive except in becoming human. Even though symbolic communication is unique to man, our use of nonverbal forms powers the beginning and the direction of socialization and enculturation, thus performing the role of defining the limits of behavior that can be coped with and thereby establishing a finite world.

What then of man's entrance into civilization five thousand years ago and his entrance into the phenomenal world of civilization today? If our proposition that the recognition of infinite possibility is more and more forced into our consciousness by the increasing individuation of phenomena can we continue to utilize the human adaptation of nonverbal communication in tribal and peasant cultures to achieve the meaningful whole?—namely, by surpressing infinite possibility? These are not civilizational means. If the means are not civilizational, how can its demand be met when the immanence of infinite possibility is always present and if the consciousness of it is increasingly likely in the specification of culture and act in civilization? We as creatures of civilization are more and more forced to bring the recognition of infinite possibility into focus. And if the developers and those being developed consider themselves to be equipped with the only satisfactory means of dealing with civilization (family, kin, village, neighborhood), how does one deal with infinity of civilization?

In an important sense, mankind facing civilization and a country embarking on development share the encounter with man's quest for new experience, which carries with it the threat of apprehended but nonpredictable results. It is in this circumstance that the infinity of possible behavior is recognized, and it is here that we refuse its implications by setting limits on acceptable behavior. Two things are observable. First, here lies the origin of behavior which offers threats and dangers to all culturally organized societies. Second, and possibly more important, there is tacit and usually nonverbalized recognition of potential for behavior along with the dangers to the integration of the individual personality and society this carries, for we have only ephemeral glimpses of what the new behavior might be. That which is real but incomplete can by this very fact constitute, in relation to the culture being employed, a foreshadowing of behavioral reality uncontrolled. By its as yet incompleteness, its nonhuman character but human partialities, it is an unknown threat to all men. Yet civilizational culture by its constant insistence on discreteness of events forces man into the conscious recognition of their existence and into the apprehension that behavior may be subject to infinite choice. For man, civilized or developing, such a circumstance is intolerable. An experiential world without high predictability, hence not a world of limited choice and limited behavior that permits a holistic treatment of experience, our tribal and village cultural past has taught us is not in the nature of human being. Infinity laid bare exposes a yammering idiocy that lurks on the edges of cognition.

Here we have defined civilization as a cultural form in which an infinity of choice in behavior is brought to conscious consideration. This potential is easily forgotten in smaller cultural worlds. The maximal sharing of culture there brings little need for conscious choice-making of the sort implied for civilization. The specification of events and individuals make such a condition potentially more consciously held while we refuse it. We recoil from its implications and retreat into a more restricted and predictable world. I suspect this retreat is not only to peasant and tribal levels of understanding but, because of its primary dependence on nonverbal communication, to something we might term the "australopithecine cuddle."

The burden of the foregoing is that men of civilization gain their primary identification, and hence their definition of *human* and the values attached thereto, from modes of learning and cultural organization that are not civilizational. Although of civilization, the *human* goals of the developer are usually couched in noncivilizational terms. This is so despite conscious efforts to avoid ethnocentrism, national aims, and to gain international good will and all the rest. Even the definitions of human devised by international professional bodies emphasize primary group identity—something akin to kin. In effect, what the developer is saying is: "Come into my village and see how to live in civilization."[1] And let us not be self-indulgent by shrugging on cultural hair shirts and beating our breasts before the world crying "mea culpa." The developing countries will receive civilization with the same expectation but this time their village.

At base, the instigation and the reception of change and development use basic values and cultural premises of nonverbal transmission as the ultimate goal in any such program. Sophisticated developers, planners, and instigators of these processes wish to present change in these terms. But the seeking of such goals, let alone achieving them, is based on two almost incompatible assumptions: first, that the receivers of directed culture change can accommodate modern civilization on this basis; second, and still worse, that these as vehicles of development and directed culture change can be used to transmit modern civilization. What is presented is a western European peasant view of civilization, not civilization. Two peasantries do not make a civilization.

While the developer may be a peasant at heart, he brings with him all the trappings of civilization. The developing culture then undergoes the process of learning the implications of civilization. Its members encounter the terror of the formlessness of exposed infinity. They achieve realization, once exposed to history, of the systematic storage of experience and of the infinitely developing knowledge systems, so that the anchors of certainty and ultimate truth no longer lie within the grasp of maturation.

The problem is disturbing. One is tempted to fall back on the metaphor of the blind leading the blind. But we need to ask whether or not the five-thousand year refusal of civilization is not an indicator of success in coping with the phenomenon. Is such complexity best dealt with by misdirection and the insistence upon the referral of human problems to a level more suited to our definitions of reality? But does modern civilization create a condition in which it is more and more impossible to refuse history? Is the increasing universalization of modern civilization of such potential firsthand experience that it will be difficult to conceive any other environment? The counter-active positions of greater individuation of the person and experience on the one hand, and the modern refusal of history in the form of "existentialism" on the other, may simply be the continuation of the process started long ago.

It is in this context that we should briefly explore the significance of the shift from the search for "scientific law" of the nineteenth and early twentieth centuries to a concern for "process." Has this occurred because process does not demand a statement about the totality of things and a means of coping with it? Or need not process concern itself with the whole, for it is ineffably existential in counter-position to civilization which so emphasizes past and future that the present is meaningless. I think the concern with process may be an updating of our past refusal of history and civilization. Process may be the means of coping with civilization without coping. If process is all, one achieves the ultimate reduction in human behavior. We become no longer concerned with unlimited or limited possibilities but instead only with an intense *what is*. The universal, timeless truth is achieved on a rational, conscious level. Civilization is superseded. And in this sophisticated and worldly retreat to kin and village have we found a means of dealing with civilization? Systems theory may be the new messiah.

It has been the burden of this essay that the underlying value systems concerning the ultimate worth and necessity of human being, no matter the cultural bias present, are premised on modes of life in which small, intimate groups are basically "human." The desirable state of man is that in which firsthand experience and affiliation are the necessary bases of all social activity, hence more than linguistic communication is involved. An attempt has been made to demonstrate the inadequacy of such an assumption in civilizational culture.

The persistent query is: How then can man cope with civilization?

We are highly successful family creatures and village dwellers. Perhaps the seemingly universal aspects of human life such as childhood, adolescence, marriage, territorial identification, empathetic understanding, and all those social phenomena basically derived through nonverbal communication are merely the present-day practice of primate and simian traditions in tribal and village dress. I suspect the answer, if it comes, will be defined as nonhuman. Not in the fashion usual to us because it is of a different culture, but because it will represent a new level of integration in behavioral evolution.

NOTES

1. I am indebted to Professor Norma McLeod for this metaphor.

REFERENCES

Count, Earl W., 1958-1959. Eine biologische Entwicklungsgeschichte der menschlichen Sozialität. *Homo* 9:126-146; 10:1-35, 65-92.

————, 1968. An Essay on Phasia: On the Phylogenesis of Man's Speech Function. *Homo* 18:170-227.

————, 1969. Animal Communication in Man-Science: An Essay in Perspective. In *Approaches to Animal Communication*, Thomas A. Sebeok and Alexandra Ramsay, ed. (The Hague: Mouton), pp. 71-130.

Redfield, Robert, 1953. *The Primitive World and Its Transformation* (Ithaca, N. Y.: Cornell University Press).

The Role of Education in Bringing About Change

WILFRID C. BAILEY

A culture may be viewed as a stream of behavior running through time and space. Actually a culture is composed of individuals, at various points in their life cycles, following more or less predictable patterns of behavior. Each of these individuals enters the culture at some point in time, usually through birth, and learns to live in it. Eventually each leaves it, usually through death, but the culture continues on. The important point is that in order to satisfy his needs each individual must and does learn enough of the culture in which he lives. It is true that he may not master all of the culture and that his needs may never be fully satisfied, but there are minimum levels of learning that must be attained in order for him to function as a member of society.

This learning process is never left to chance. Each culture has developed means of insuring that each new individual will acquire those elements that make him a predictable member of society. Although this process is not always complete, a minimum level of success is necessary for perpetuating the culture. This process of learning one's culture is called enculturation. When there are formal or special institutional structures to carry out this task, it is education. There are many forms of the educational process, of which a school is only one.

Learning is a lifelong process, although most of it takes place in the early years, and this early learning influences later learning. The individual's role in education changes through his life cycle. In the early years the individual is primarily a receiver of culture, a learner; as he grows older he may become a dispenser of culture, a teacher. In a culture where older children take care of their younger siblings, the two roles overlap. Adults are primarily in a teacher

31

role in relationship to children. In some cases children may instruct adults. However, studies of programs such as vocational agriculture show that the transmission to their parents of what children learn in school is rather limited—any teen-ager will tell you that it does not take a scientific study to demonstrate this point.

Herskovits points out that early learning is primarily unconscious, while later learning is conscious (Herskovits 1948). The young child is not fully aware that he is being subjected to a process of cultural transmission. As he grows older he becomes more aware that he is learning. There is another important age differential that is related to what is learned. Early learning tends to be for the perpetuation of the culture. Later learning is apt to result in culture change or alteration of the pattern learned earlier. The cultural elements learned in later life frequently come from other cultures. With this point of view, enculturation is learning one's original or first culture. Later learning may be learning a second culture. This is a part of the process of acculturation.

In a culture undergoing change the relationship between enculturation and acculturation is rather complex. (1) When the culture of the school and the pupil are the same the process is enculturation. (2) When the culture of the school and the pupil are different the process is acculturation. (3) When the initial education is conducted by teachers of another culture it is enculturation for the child but acculturation for the culture. A case in point would be where scientific agriculture is taught in a peasant village school by agricultural experts from outside the village. If this takes place at the time when a boy in the village would normally have learned about farming from his father, he is being enculturated because this is his first cultural experience. However, the end result is alteration of the traditional culture of the village because of outside cultural influences. Thus the village is acculturated. (4) When adults are educated in order to make up for what was missed in the regular or expected educational process it is continued or delayed enculturation. A literacy program for adults who dropped out of school in the first few years or who never went to the village school is enculturation because these adults are learning something that they should have learned much earlier. (5) When adult education introduces new skills not already present in the culture, the process is acculturation. An example would be a literacy program is introduced into a preliterate Indian group living on the headwaters of the Amazon. (6) The educational process may be enculturation for some and acculturation for others in the same classroom. Middle class children under a middle class teacher are being enculturated. However, the same material may represent an alien culture to the lower class children and for them the result is acculturation. (7) The educational process in the classroom may be both enculturation and acculturation for the pupils. The well-known school at Rough Rock on the Navajo reservation includes in its instruction many elements of traditional Navajo culture along with a curriculum introduced from the dominant American culture.

This paper takes the position that culture change is usually the result of something learned from the outside. This point of view goes back at least as far as Ralph Linton (1936). He attempted to demonstrate that only a relatively minor part of culture was the result of events internal to the culture. Further, change today is apt to be deliberate rather than accidental. Change is planned. In other words, much modern change is the result of an educational process designed to bring about change. It is a part of man's expanding efforts to control his environment. The neolithic revolution gave man increasing control over his food supply; he began to manipulate his natural environment. The development of formal programs for cultural change is a way of exerting deliberate control over the cultural environment.

In the following pages I will examine two sets of factors related to the role of education in bringing about change. First, I will look at a number of problems associated with educational programs for change. Second, I will discuss the question of bringing about change within the educational programs themselves.

Developmental change has received much attention from social philosophers and social scientists since World War II. Concern over the growing disparity between the well-being of most of the people in the developed nations and that of the great masses in the underdeveloped countries has stimulated investigation of problems accompanying the process of social change in which a whole society moves toward development. However, the study of developmental change actually goes back to the days when England was struggling through the industrial revolution. Adam Smith published *An Inquiry into the Nature and Causes of the Wealth of Nations* in 1776. He was followed by David Ricardo, Thomas Robert Malthus, Karl Marx, and others.

Development is universally thought of in terms of economic growth, with population, social structure, and political organization as associated variables. Anthropological theory has reflected this same point of view. The cultural evolutionists, for example, have used material culture as indicators of development—Marvin Harris (1968) examines all of the history of anthropology from this perspective.

Of concern to us here is the role of education in developmental change. Although much of the thinking has focused on development as primarily an economic problem, the role of education has been recognized to some extent. Marx pointed out that when the means of production were controlled by a select few, popular education was retarded. Recently, many have directly investigated the role between education and development. Harbison and Myers (1964) attempted to show that development necessarily involves educational advance as well as economic growth. By examining the cases of England, Japan, and Russia, Adams and Bjork (1969:20-46) tested the proposition that education was necessary for economic development. They concluded that in England changes in education came irregularly and did not fit well with the curve of economic development. On the other hand, development in Japan and Russia followed closely with improvement in education. In Japan compulsory education was introduced within a few years after the Meiji Restoration, and universal formal primary education was achieved within fifty years after the developmental process had begun. The Education Law of 1872 stated that "every man only after learning diligently each according to his capacity will be able to increase his property and prosper in his business" (Dairoku 1909:68-69). Adams and Bjork conclude that

it is, of course, possible that, although education is presently crucial to the developed societies, it played little or no part in beginning or accelerating the process of development. And it is also possible that even if education played little part in the advancement of the presently developed world, it may still be of great significance in the developmental process of the many societies now striving to break out of old patterns. (1969:23)

It would seem that while growth, both economic and educational, was slow in England, the end result was the modern industrial city whose existence is dependent on a relatively high level of education. Therefore nations attempting to enter rapidly into a modern developed economy must quickly acquire a skilled literate population. The reasons are several. Production and trade are almost wholly monetarized, requiring bookkeeping, information gathering and storing, complex contractual arrangements, and so on. An extraordinarily large number of crucial communications are in written form rather than oral form. Political and economic organization demands a system of written law enforceable throughout the nation. Dependence on advanced technology is absolute. Demographic balance must be established, and this is rarely achieved without a high average education (Adams and Bjork 1962:21-23).

Recognition of the need for education as a prerequisite for modernization is not new. The problem of education came up early in the era of colonialism. The concern was twofold. The colonial governments sought both to maintain order and to produce raw materials for the growing industries back home. Most of the early education, particularly in Africa, was introduced by missionaries (Wilson 1963). Conversion of the heathens involved teaching them to read the Bible and catechism, but education beyond this level was limited. A small number received technical training in skills needed to maintain and operate mission stations, government agencies, plantations, mines, and various business enterprises. The French and Portuguese attempted to Westernize completely a select few. These *asimilados*, to use the Portuguese term, were given citizenship and used as a cadre to help govern the native population of the colony.

Universal education beyond primary literacy training for native peoples in colonial areas did not become an objective until the modern period. Programs in the underdeveloped areas have shifted from the development of a colony as a resource for the economic progress of the European power to the development of the newly independent nations for the benefit of all its inhabitants. Because of the recognition of the relationship between education and economic growth, schools have become a major element in development programs. Almost all such programs either directly or indirectly include improvement of the general level of education and training in special skills.

Concepts of underdevelopment and poverty are relative terms. An underdeveloped country is one in which the average material well-being of its inhabitants is appreciably inferior to that of developed countries (Buchanan and Ellis 1955:3-4). The usual standard of measure is the per capita real income of Canada, Australia, Western Europe, and the United States. Within the United States itself there have been a number of attempts to set up standards of measure in terms of a minimum income figure (Bailey 1960:60-61). This figure changes from time to time and is based on establishing an income level necessary to purchase basic necessities of life.

Inhabitants of underdeveloped nations, underdeveloped areas of the United States, and inhabitants of urban slums share many characteristics associated with poverty. These include limited education, disease, high death rate, high birth rate, low level of living, malnutrition, poor credit facilities, and weak feelings of cohesion with the dominant culture. People exhibiting these characteristics are often unable to contribute strength to developmental growth, and a vicious circle is established from which escape is difficult. There is, furthermore, an external factor operating: the "good things in life" and access routes to obtain them are usually controlled by a powerful, literate elite (Curle 1969:40). All of this contributes to what Oscar Lewis described as a culture of poverty (Lewis 1966).

The discussion of the role of education in developmental change should therefore not be limited to overseas programs. There are many parallels between the educational problems of underdeveloped nations and those facing rural and urban poverty groups in the United States. Lessons learned in developing countries can be applied here at home, and work with domestic problems can have relevance to international developmental education (De'Ath 1969). The basic problems faced by these educational programs can be grouped under three headings: Who shall be educated? Who shall control education? What shall be taught?

Who shall be educated? It is always the case that there are only limited resources that can be utilized for education. It is axiomatic that in underdeveloped societies, where the need is the greatest, the means are the least. Complete universal education can not be provided immediately. Hard decisions must therefore be made in the allocation of available funds. The problem goes beyond designation of a portion of national resources that will go to education. For example, target groups must be identified.

The first basic decision is whether to start at the top or at the bottom of the educational system. Because costs per student increase rapidly when advanced education is provided the decision becomes one of providing either limited training for a large number of students or a high level of education for a limited group. Belgium attempted to achieve universal literacy in the Congo but provided little for advanced training. As a result there were only ten college graduates at the time of independence. England attempted to provide for a trained cadre which could take over the reins, so that when independence came, thousands of Nigerians were attending college abroad. Most Nigerians, however, had only limited schooling.

Some development educators see universal education as the vital key for all other forms of development. This is the basic philosophy of community development programs. National advancement can be achieved only if the proper foundation is established. One of the important ingredients in this base is that of literacy as a gateway not only to obtaining technical skills but also to playing a role in the political decision-making processes.

At the other extreme are educators who see preuniversity education as having a negligible role in change and development (Braithwaite 1967). There are several arguments for the position that development must start at the top. First, even if it is valid to assume that development will take place by itself when the population mass reaches the proper stage, this process is painfully slow and the need for development too urgent. Second, it is the cosmopolitan, university-educated person rather than the local product of the village school who has a workable understanding of what is required for improving the life of people. It is the educated elite who can make the decisions and quickly bring about change. Third, developing nations and groups see a modern university as a symbol of the modern world. A beautiful university campus, a nationally based airline with jets landing at a modern airport, and a variety of spacious public buildings are used to help establish identity with the developed nations. A disproportionate share of limited funds will be used for such enterprises while more critical needs are neglected.

Research has not clearly determined which educational strategy has the greatest results. Anderson (1961) examined two dozen countries. Although it is usually assumed that a productive economy requires a high level of education and a large number of highly educated elite, development of an advanced economy did not necessarily result in increasing proportions of students moving up from the disadvantaged sectors of the population. Specific ideologies and education policies that impinge uniquely on each social group peculiar to each nation appear to be behind the results found. Information is needed on how training in needed skills and different patterns of utilizing human resources can accomplish equivalent results.

Another dimension in the selection of the group to be educated is age. The usual distinction is between early childhood education and adult education. Headstart and Follow Through education programs in this country are based on the assumption that some children do not have certain early learning experiences that prepare them to benefit from formal education. Other programs are aimed at adults, and in fact, most development programs include adult education (Prosser 1967). The Agricultural Extension Service in the United States, which was established in 1914, is one of the most extensive adult education programs in the world and has provided the model for programs in many other parts of the world. However, DeVries (1961) suggests that adolescents (boys and girls ages fourteen to eighteen) are a particularly important target group. A large proportion of effort, time, and money spent on primary education will be lost unless programs assist adolescents in moving into adult spheres utilizing the new techniques. This may be the critical point at which the vicious cycle of the culture of poverty may be broken.

Special attention needs to be placed on education for girls and women. In the early stages of development of formal education programs, girls usually have fewer chances than boys, partly because of the fear of coeducation among parents and partly because the economic importance of school-education for girls is much less obvious. The role of women as a catalyzing force for culture change is often overlooked. Women take care of the homes, and their skill level largely determines the quality of life in the family. In addition, women are usually responsible for the preschool training of children; they are bearers of culture.

Although scarce resources seem to dictate selection of a particular group as the target for education, this concentration can be the cause of certain problems. Increased education can result in the formation of social classes based on education. One rather common phenomenon in developing nations is that the educated elite lose contact with traditional culture. Although they leave home with the desire to obtain an education and then return home to apply what they have learned to local development, few actually do so. They acquire modern patterns of living, and returning to their underdeveloped homelands means returning to an inferior life style. To a certain extent returning is a sign of failure and loss of newly achieved status.

As a result, basic education for the masses and advanced education for a select few creates two separate groups. In Sub-Saharan Africa, tribal groups often look upon the educated elite as "black white men." Lack of educational balance between sexes creates another problem. Where higher education is restricted to one sex it often makes for marital difficulties. Many educated African men find it almost impossible to find a wife with their level of education. For the same reason, the female schoolteacher in the Spanish peasant village is faced with the problem of finding a husband of her intellectual level.

Who shall control education? Generally speaking, formal education in the colonies and in developing nations has been introduced from outside. However, this is a somewhat ethnocentric point of view. It ignores the basic fact that every culture has a system of transmitting culture to its children. Some of these systems include a type of school often referred to as the bush school. The Ngoni of Malawi are very conscious of training their young people and are somewhat resentful of claims that mission schools introduced education. They feel that they had their own education system and that this system was disrupted, first by the mission schools and then by the government schools. Margaret Read (1968:2-3) illustrates the changes in views of education in her report of a conversation between two young Ngoni schoolteachers and a senior chief. The chief speaks first:

"How is your school?"

"The classes are full and the children are learning well, *Inkosi.*

"How do they behave?"

"Like Ngoni children, *Inkosi.*"

"What do they learn?"

"They learn reading, writing, arithmetic, scripture, geography and drill, *Inkosi.*"

"Is that education?"

"It is education, *Inkosi.*"

"No! No! No! Education is very broad, very deep. It is not only in the books, it is learning how to live. I am an old man now. When I was a boy I went with the Ngoni army to the war against the Bemba. Then the mission came and I went to school. I became a teacher. Then I was a chief. Then the government came. I have seen the country change, and now there are many schools and many young men go away to work to find money. I tell you that Ngoni children must learn to work and earn money. Do you hear?"

"*Yebo, Inkosi.*" (Yes, O Chief).

The control of the schools boils down to two fundamental issues. First, should the control be local, or should schools be administered by some external agency? Second, if schools are introduced from the outside, should they be the work of missionaries, a national education agency, or in some cases an international agency, either private or governmental (Zack 1966)? The grass roots community development approach in which local decision-making is a primary target has become basic in many programs for developmental change. Schools are usually included in these programs. One such example of this is the Navaho, who are deeply involved not only in the Rough Rock school, and the community college at Many Farms, but also now in the high school at Ramah. Furthermore, Follow-Through programs on the reservations, although originating from the outside, involve the tribal officials and the parents. The whole problem of Bureau of Indian Affairs versus tribal control has become a major issue on more than one reservation (Peterson and Richburg 1970).

The first schools in many areas were established by missionaries. In Africa in particular the mission schools have remained a major factor in education up to the present time, and in some areas they are still the only schools. At independence the majority of African countries found themselves with educational systems managed by religious groups. For example, in Kenya on the eve of independence the government had only 8 primary schools and no secondary schools for Africans. A total of 40,024 primary schools and 50 secondary schools received government aid, and the overwhelming majority of these were managed by religious groups (Scanlon 1966:17). From the time of the earliest Portuguese missionaries in the fifteenth century through the nineteenth century, Christian missions and education were inextricably bound together. It should be remembered, however, that in Europe and in the United States the educational system also had its origins in religious groups and philanthropic organizations. Most of the older universities in the United States were originally church-related. Until very recently, schools for blacks in the South were affiliated with churches. Public education run by government, therefore, is a rather recent development, and most European countries still have government support for a dual school system. It is mainly in the United States that there has been an effort to maintain a rigid separation between state and church education. The dominant position of mission schools in the former colonial areas is therefore a retention of a system that was once the common pattern in Europe.

Related to the problem of control of the educational system is control of the teachers. In the early mission schools all teachers were Europeans or Americans. The entrance of indigenous people into teaching has been slow. Most of the native teachers have been poorly trained and have taught in the primary grades. College graduates tended to go into government positions rather than education; as a result, poorly trained native teachers often helped to maintain the gulf between those who received primary education and the select few who went on to more advanced schooling. Now the great need is for adequately trained native teachers who can bridge the gap between traditional and modern cultures.

What should be taught? Curriculum is a major source of controversy among the schools in developing areas. Because of the many mission schools there is the question of the proper blend of religious and secular training. Another problem centers around the proper balance of technical and academic courses. There is a vital need for vocational training both to equip students for finding jobs and to provide increased skill levels to man the developing economy. But since education has been one of the major routes for upward mobility into high-status government jobs, the more ambitious students usually want academic rather than vocational education.

Various systems of accreditation force schools that are able to offer only a single track program to concentrate on a program that will permit entrance into the next highest level of instruction. This has been a source of difficulty in American schools where the need for vocational training is the greatest. In the British colonies a parallel problem was created by the external examination system. The secondary schools and colleges were associated with one or another of the schools in England. Students in the colonial schools took the same examinations as the students in England. They were required to have a high level of knowledge about England but were allowed to know next to nothing about their own country. American Indians and blacks have the same complaint about their schools today. Newly independent nations in Africa are attempting to remedy this situation by establishing African examination systems. This is a slow process because those responsible for developing the new examinations were all trained under the old system.

Probably the most critical problem in the development of curriculum is the choice of the language of instruction. Very often instruction is carried out in the standard form of a major language different from the native family language of the students. This condition is sometimes found where there are minority groups or where a colonial government was once in force. Because of the mutually unintelligible languages, the people are frequently forced to use the language of the colonial power as the lingua franca. Where there are several native languages it would be impossible to foster any one of them as the lingua franca because the speakers of that language would be in a privileged position and there would be strong opposition from the speakers of other languages (Hindmarsh 1966:161).

In Tanzania the language of instruction at the primary level was the local tribal language. Swahili was used as soon as possible where it was not the mother tongue. English was introduced as a foreign language in the third year and was the language of instruction in the upper primary school. Thus a child had three different languages of instruction before completing primary school (Herrick 1968:151). The preparation of curriculum materials and the training of teachers are most difficult in cases such as this. Even when materials are translated into the various languages, publishers are reluctant to handle them. There are relatively few well-trained multilingual teachers, particularly among those able to teach in the local tribal languages.

When both the teacher and the students use one of the major languages the problems are still not over. There are both standard and nonstandard versions of the languages. For example, five different types of English have been identified in Sierra Leone. These are (1) standard English, spoken chiefly by expatriates; (2) a regional dialect closely approximating a West African form of English; (3) Krio, an English-based Creole spoken as a mother language; (4) West African Pidgin English; and (5) marginal languages spoken between expatriates and their servants (Tiffen 1968:101). In the United States there are various forms of nonstandard English spoken by various minority groups including southern Negroes (Stewart 1970), various American Indian groups, and Chicanos.

Under conditions of change the child in the classroom may be faced with the problem of dealing with several languages. This can range from bilingualism (two different languages), to biglossia (high and low forms of the same language), to bidialectal speech (coexistence and complementary use of a national standard language and a local or regional dialect) (Lounsbury 1961:309-313).

The solution is not to eliminate the language differences. Retention of one's language can be the last symbol of a culture that is slipping away. A man's language is his most intimate possession and the badge of membership in his group. To stigmatize a child's native language alienates him from his family without bringing him into the dominant culture (McDavid 1964).

Here in the United States we can see some of the problems faced in many nations, particularly in the modernizing areas of the world. The American stereotype has been the "melting pot" theory; the notion of cultural pluralism has not been part of the American dream. It came as a shock, therefore, to discover that there are people who do not want to lose their cultural heritage and speak of self-determination as an alternative to the forced melting pot (John and Horner 1970). A crucial question may be whether the goal of economic opportunity for all carries with it the price of becoming a monocultural society. There are those who argue that the United States is a polycultural society with monocultural schools, and this is a damaging inequity forced on the poverty child (Williams 1970).

Since the role of education in change is so often the introduction of new ideas from more developed areas, the question becomes one of acculturation versus biculturalism. Should the pupil be taught the dominant culture as a substitute for his original cultural training? Or should he be taught a second culture in such a way as to be able to function in it while at the same time retaining and continuing to live in his original culture? Some educators are convinced that most of the scholastic difficulties of students of minority groups stem from a feeling of alienation resulting from pressure for acculturation, and that bicultural education would do much to relieve this problem.

Various schemes of bicultural education have been developed, one of the most famous being the Navaho's Rough Rock Demonstration School previously mentioned. Efforts to evaluate these programs have been inconclusive—it has been difficult to demonstrate that in the long run the result is really any better. Perhaps the real value comes in greater retention of students, greater involvement of the local population, and a generally more favorable attitude toward education.

In periods of change, institutionalized education must prepare to change more significantly than its society. Too often it is the very institution of education that helps maintain the lack of change (Carse 1970:117). It is clear that education must shift radically its approach to people and to knowledge if it is to become an important factor in culture change. Two places where it is particularly essential that changes occur are in the attitudes of teachers and in the structure of education.

Changing the attitudes of teachers is not easy. Part of the problem is related to the use of the teaching profession as an aid to upward mobility. "If Dick and Jane are middle-class, the teacher is even more so. Even worse, many teachers are suspected of having *lower* middle class backgrounds, which means that they have been through a struggle for upward mobility which has desensitized them to the problems of the poor and the culturally different" (Coombs 1970:64). I observed teachers on one Indian reservation and found that the one teacher who appeared to be the most rigid in keeping all elements of Indian culture out of her classroom was a member of the tribe who had come back to teach after having received college training off the reservation. If teachers continue to act as the sole possessors of knowledge and to evaluate their pupils in terms of this knowledge we can expect little change. The teacher must be a constant learner and be willing to learn from and about his pupils (Carse 1970:124).

While some teachers can be criticized for maintaining the status quo and remaining oblivious to the need for change, others can be seen as overly zealous in their desire to institute change. The role of the school to create change sometimes gives a messianic role to teachers which they are not trained to understand. Some teachers overcome this deficiency by personal sensitivity, dedication, modesty, and example while others run head-on into cultural resistance and become discouraged and defeated (Belshaw 1970:14).

The basic attitudes of teachers in dealing with cultures other than their own can be seen in the rise in the use of three terms: culturally deprived, culturally disadvantaged, and culturally different. Teachers, with their middle-class or colonial-power background, at first saw children as coming to school from homes lacking many things common to the teacher's background. Standardized testing procedures led to the erroneous conclusion that the children had an insufficient or underdeveloped capacity to learn. They failed to take into account the discrepancy between the students' cultural backgrounds and the cultural background assumed in standardized tests. This gave rise to the term "culturally deprived."

The concept of cultural deprivation assumes that certain individuals have not acquired a full complement of culture. The result is the "vacuum approach": the child arrives not knowing anything, and this void must be filled. For example, the lower-class Negro family consisting of a mother and her children with a series of husbands or male friends, when viewed from a middle-class model, is a disorganized family or no family (Deutsch 1963). Yet recent examination of the lower-class Negro family has revealed that it is not disorganized but in reality exhibits a very consistent pattern of behavior. It is actually a special type of family, not at all lacking in organization (Gonzales 1969). Further, efforts to describe linguistic deficiencies of Negro children have revealed that their speech patterns are fully consistent. Such patterns of nonstandard English do not represent a lack of language but a language dialect.

The recognition of nonstandard behavior of groups in the classroom as representative of subcultures rather than nonculture or disorganized culture has led to other terms to replace that of "culturally deprived." One of these is "culturally disadvantaged," which term expresses a willingness to allow the presence of subcultures but makes a value judgment. The implication is that the cultural background of the children places them at a disadvantage in particular situations. The basic assumption is that the existing cultural patterns among the students must be replaced by those of the teacher representing the dominating culture.

A more nearly neutral term to apply to cultural variation is "culturally different." This term takes the position that although the child comes from a different cultural background, no value judgment is made concerning "correctness." Various solutions are then possible, including the retention or reinforcement of the "different" culture in such a way as to overcome problems growing out of competing in a multicultural situation. Although this is the most popular approach today, there are certain dangers. Recognition of the legitimacy of the minority culture should not be an excuse for doing nothing. To overromanticize the traditional culture can retard adjustments needed to cope with long-range changes taking place in the world that are beyond the control of the individuals concerned.

Changing the structure of education may be a precondition for its assuming an effective role as a change agent. At the present time little is known about the social, cultural, and psychological climates favorable for developmental planning in the educational sector. For example, in Red China the achievement motivation has led to the idea that "to learn, to modernize, and to increase productivity is the responsibility of every citizen" (Adams 1970:193-194). In India it is assumed that the decline in the rigidity of the caste system is leading to a new pattern in the availability of education, which has greatly increased the interest in education and the willingness to make changes. India attempted to use a community development plan to bring about change. A corps of village-level workers would each work with a group of ten villages. However, with nearly half a million villages, implementation of this program required a vast force of workers, and it was necessary to establish a whole series of schools to train the workers before they could take up their task of adult education in the villages.

Do the educational systems in modernizing nations develop through a series of stages? Beeby (1966) attempted to identify a series of four such stages. They begin with a stage in which the teachers are both poorly educated and poorly trained and move to the stage where they are well educated and well trained. During this transition there is movement away from a rigid externally designed curriculum toward a pattern that is both flexible and relevant to the situation. Yet there is a built-in danger. The inescapable framework of worldwide modernization leaves no alternative but to adopt a formal educational system to provide technical training. Yet efforts to acclimatize education more completely to local cultures threatens to stultify the income-raising potentialities of education without which other benefits cannot appear. Further, is it necessary for each individual society to pass through these same steps or is it possible to skip one or more and move directly into the more effective stage?

Finally, how does educational innovation take place? There have been many efforts to study adoption of new educational practices. Beginning in the 1930s Paul R. Mort began the study of adapability of educational systems (Mort 1946). Most of the recent studies have attempted to apply to education the pattern of stages worked out by rural sociologists in the study of the adoption of new agricultural practices (Miles 1964; Richburg 1969). A study of school bond elections in Iowa failed to find any conclusive relationship between demographic characteristics of communities and the success or failure of school bond issues. Districts with successful votes usually passed the next and converse (Beal, Lagomarcino, and Hartman 1966). This seems to indicate a need for anthropological studies in community settings to identify cultural variables associated with various types of educational change.

It is clear, then, that education plays an important role in bringing about change. Yet its role performance is plagued with many critical problems. First, there are critical decisions related to how education can best be used in the process of worldwide modernization. These include who shall be educated, who shall control education, and what should be taught. Second, it is obvious that if education is to be utilized successfully as an instrument for change, changes in education itself are necessary. Changes are needed in the attitudes of educators and in the structure of education.

Modernization is taking place at an ever accelerating rate. There is a great urgency and a need for speed, yet education is a slow process. A child is born without culture, and a healthy, normal child can learn any culture. Yet this learning takes many years. In theory the individual child can jump from the most traditional tribal culture to the most advanced through the process of enculturation and education, but cultures as a whole change slowly. It is impractical to remove at birth a whole generation from their parents in order to enculturate them completely into a new culture. Even more important is the ethical question, whether we have the right to change the culture of another, and if so, to what extent.

Much has been said about the relationship between education and developmental change; many statistics have been compiled. But examination of the literature reveals that most of the writing has been done by educators and that there has been very little real research on the processes involved. Although Solon Kimball and George Spindler, in the United States, and Margaret Read, in England, have been writing on education for many years, there has been relatively little interest in the anthropology of education. Recently the field of anthropology of education has shown great vigor and development (Sindell 1969). The Council on Anthropology and Education of the American Anthropological Association has assumed a primary role in stimulating discussion and research. What is needed is the development of better conceptual systems that would be applicable to partial societies such as schools and classrooms (Spindler 1971). In addition these partial societies need to be understood in terms of the larger society and the total process of modernization.

Relevancy is now a magic word, and applied anthropology has become legitimate as a tool for the betterment of mankind. It is more than the simple application of anthropological knowledge but requires research on changes in human behavior believed to ameliorate contemporary social, economic, and technical problems facing the world today (Foster 1969). The demands for better research methods and investigation of real, ongoing situations will enrich our body of anthropological data and result in more adequate theories of society and change. The field of anthropology of education and its application to the study of developmental change has a bright future.

REFERENCES

Adams, Don, 1970. *Education and Modernization in Asia* (Reading, Mass.: Addison-Wesley).
————, and Robert M. Bjorks, 1969. *Education in Developing Areas* (New York: David McKay).
Anderson, C. Arnold, 1961. Access to Higher Education and Economic Development. In *Education, Economy, and Society*, A. H. Halsey, Jean Floud, and C. Arnold Anderson, eds. (New York: Free Press), pp. 252-265.
Bailey, Wilfrid C., 1960. Rural Development and the Social Sciences. *Sociologia* 22:52-70.
Beal, George M., Virgil Lagomarcino, and John J. Hartman, 1966. *Iowa School Bond Issues* (Ames, Iowa: Iowa State University).
Beeby, Clarence Edward, 1966. *The Quality of Education in Developing Countries* (Cambridge, Mass.: Harvard University Press).
Belshaw, Cyril S., 1971. Anthropology, Development, and Education. *Council on Anthropology and Education Newsletter* 1 (2):11-14.
Braithwaite, E. W., 1967. Education, Social Change, and the New Zealand Economy. *New Zealand Journal of Educational Studies* 2:32-62.
Buchanan, Norman S., and Howard S. Ellis, 1955. *Approaches to Economic Development* (New York: Twentieth Century Fund).
Carse, William, 1970. Teacher Education in Culture Change. In *Culture Change, Mental Health, and Poverty*, Joseph C. Finney, ed. (New York: Simon and Schuster), pp. 117-124.
Coombs, L. Madison, 1970. *The Educational Disadvantage of the Indian American Student.* Clearing House on Rural Education and Small Schools (Las Cruces, N.M.: New Mexico State University).
Curle, Adam, 1969. *Educational Problems of Developing Societies* (New York: Frederick A. Praeger).
Dairoku, Kikuchi, 1909. *Japanese Education* (London: J. Murray).
Dakin, Julian, 1968. Language and Education in India. In *Language in Education: The Problem in Commonwealth Africa and the Indo-Pakistan Sub-continent,* Julian Dakin, Brian Tiffen, and H. G. Widdowson, eds. (London: Oxford University Press), pp. 1-62.
De'Ath, Colin, 1969. *Black Education in the United States and Its Relevance to International Development Education.* International and Development Education Program Occasional Paper (Pittsburgh: University of Pittsburgh).
DeVries, Egbert, 1961. Man in Rapid Social Change (Garden City: Doubleday).
Deutsch, Martin, 1963. The Disadvantaged Child and the Learning Process. In *Education in Depressed Areas*, A. Harry Passow, ed. (New York: Teachers College Press, Columbia University).
Foster, George M., 1969. *Applied Anthropology* (Boston: Little, Brown).
Gonzales, Nancie L. Solien, 1969. *Black Carib Household Structure* (Seattle: University of Washington Press).

Harbison, Frederick H., and Charles A. Myers, 1964. *Education, Manpower, and Economic Growth* (New York: McGraw-Hill).

Harris, Marvin, 1968. *The Rise of Anthropological Theory: A History of Theories of Culture* (New York: Thomas Y. Crowell).

Herrick, Allison Butler, Sidney A. Harrison, Howard J. John, Susan McKnight, and Barbara Skapa, 1968. *Area Handbook on Tanzania.* Dept. of the Army Pamphlet No. 550-62 (Washington D.C.: G.P.O.).

Herskovits, Melville J., 1948. *Man and His Works* (New York: Alfred A. Knopf).

Hindmarsh, Roland, 1966. Uganda. In *Church, State, and Education in Africa*, David G. Scanlon, ed. (New York: Teachers College Press, Columbia University), pp. 135-162.

John, Vera P., and Vivian M. Horner, 1970. Bilingualism and the Spanish-speaking Child. In *Language and Poverty*, Frederick Williams, ed. (Chicago: Markham), pp. 278-322.

Lewis, Oscar, 1966. The Culture of Poverty. *Scientific American* 215:19-25.

Linton, Ralph, 1926. *The Study of Man* (New York: Appleton-Century-Crofts).

Lounsbury, Floyd, 1962. Language. In *Biennial Review of Anthropology: 1961*, Bernard J. Siegal, ed. (Stanford: Stanford University Press), pp. 278-322.

McDavid, Raven I., 1964. Dialect and Discrimination. *University of Chicago Magazine.* February: pp. 4-5.

Miles, Matthew B., 1964. *Innovation in Education* (New York: Teachers College Press, Columbia University).

Mort, Paul R., 1946. *Principles of School Administration* (New York: McGraw-Hill).

Peterson, John H., Jr., and James R. Richburg, 1970. *The Mississippi Choctaws and Their Educational Program.* A Community Background Report accepted by Dr. Robert Havighurst as part of the Final Report of the National Study of American Indian Education to be distributed by ERIC-CRESS.

Prosser, Roy, 1967. *Adult Education for Developing Countries* (Nairobi: East African Publishing House).

Read, Margaret, 1968. *Children of Their Fathers: Growing Up among the Ngoni of Malawi* (New York: Holt, Rinehart and Winston).

Richburg, James R., 1969. Curriculum Diffusion: Dissemination and Adoption of Materials in the Anthropology Curriculum Project. Master's thesis, University of Georgia.

Scanlon, David G., 1966. *Church, State, and Education in Africa* (New York: Teachers College Press, Columbia University).

Sindell, Peter S., 1969. Anthropological Approaches to the Study of Education. *Review of Educational Research* 39:593-605.

Spindler, George D., 1971. Prospects in Anthropology and Education. *Council on Anthropology and Education Newsletter* 2:1-2.

Stewart, William E., 1970. Toward a History of American Negro Dialect. In *Language and Poverty*, Frederick Williams, ed. (Chicago: Markham), pp. 351-379.

Tiffen, Brian, 1968. Language and Education in Commonwealth Africa. In *Language in Education: The Problem in Commonwealth Africa and the Indo-Pakistan Sub-continent*, Julian Dakin, Brian Tiffen, and H. G. Widdowson, eds. (London: Oxford University Press), pp. 63-113.

Williams, Frederick, 1970. Some Preliminaries and Prospects. In *Language and Poverty*, Frederick Williams, ed. (Chicago: Markham), pp. 1-10.

Wilson, John. 1963. *Education and Changing West African Culture* (New York: Teachers College Press, Columbia University).

Zack, Arnold M., 1966. Developing Human Resources: A New Approach to Educational Assistance in Africa. In *Education and Training in Developing Countries: The Role of U. S. Foreign Aid*, William Y. Elliott, ed. (New York: Frederick A. Praeger).

Language, Linguistics, and Social Change: Retrospect and Prospect

Elizabeth A. Brandt

Linguistics from its inception has made a number of contributions to the study of change.[1] From the early origins of the field until the first part of this century, linguistics meant the study of the origin and diversification of the world's languages. Methods of reconstruction, the family tree model of change, and attempts to reconstruct the culture of a society from linguistic evidence all had great impact upon other fields of study such as biology and the study of evolution, philosophy, and anthropology. Aside from studies of linguistic change, however, it must be said that linguistics has added little to the study of social change as we normally think of it.

But this statement is not true for the approaches to change involving language-related studies, such as communication theory. Consequently language and linguistics have been separated in the title and in the content of this essay. The varieties of research in language and linguistics that have some relevance for change are numerous, and in order to keep the scope of this study manageable, the emphasis will be on language-related studies. It has also been necessary to exclude approaches to cultural analysis based on transformational-generative models of the Chomsky school, such as the models for religion and musical analysis which are being developed by Durbin (1970, 1971).

The outstanding characteristic of language-related research is that it takes the structure of language or a particular language as given and explores the functioning of language in a particular society or part of a society. Some practitioners in this area are anthropologists, communication engineers, sociologists, philosophers, social psychologists, and educators. Linguistic training and sophistication are not required. Important areas of language-related research are (1) com-

munication theory, (2) mass communications, (3) sociolinguistics, and
(4) semantics. The designation of sociolinguistics and semantics
as language-related approaches, rather than as linguistic approaches,
requires some justification. Some sociolinguistic studies focus on a
particular variable in the structure of a language and correlate it with
social structure, such as Labov's (1967) excellent study linking
phonological variables in New York City speech with socioeconomic
status. This particular study might well be classified as linguistic, but
the majority of sociolinguistic studies do not do this, operating
instead at a much more inclusive level of analysis, as with Bernstein's
(1967) work on restricted and elaborated codes or studies of multilingualism. In this study semantics is considered to be language-
related, because the model of language I favor considers semantics to
be an area outside of linguistics—the bridge between the structure
of language and the real world (Trager and Smith 1957).

Research which attempts to correlate linguistic structure or particular variables in the linguistic structure of a language with social
structure are also considered to be language-related. Included here
are the Sapir-Whorf hypothesis and generational stratification. (Language-related approaches have provided theories and results of the
most value to those interested in social change.)

The mathematical theory of communication originally developed
by Shannon and Weaver (1949) has provided many new insights
into the nature of human communication. This theory provides a
general model of the transmission of information. An information
source selects a message that is encoded into signals by a transmitter;
a receiver then decodes the signals so that it can recover the original
information (Smith 1966:13). The signal transmitted may be inter-
fered with by unwanted distortion called noise. Because noise may
interfere with messages, all communication systems possess redundancy. Redundancy is, in nontechnical terms, extra information or
overspecification in the signal. If noise blocks part of the signal,
redundancy insures that the message is still capable of being decoded.
The model discussed so far is a linear one. To this Wiener (1966)
has added the concept of feedback, which introduces a circular
process into the model such that messages received also affect messages sent.

Several investigators have modified this mathematical model to
handle human codes of interaction and to handle mass communication
media such as radio and television. Here theories concern themselves
with the source of the information, its medium, and the channels
through which it flows.

We begin with some theories about mass communications. Media are defined by Gerbner (1967:45) as means or vehicles capable of assuming forms that have the characteristics of messages or transmit messages. He abstracts from a number of definitions of mass media the following essential characteristics: mass media are technological agencies and corporate organizations engaged in the creation, selection, processing, and distribution of communications that are produced at speeds and in quantities possible only by mass-production methods. Mass media have the ability to create publics, define issues, provide common terms of reference, and thus allocate attention and power. Mass communication is seen as an institutionalized public acculturation process that reflects the structure of social relations and the stage of industrial development, as well as particular types of institutional and industrial organization and control. Mass media transform private views into public views and vice versa, thus bringing publics into existence that can then have an effect on social change and social policy.

Before continuing with a discussion of theories of communication, it is necessary to ask if communication is really relevant to the study of change, and if it is, in what ways? The ready answer is of course that it is relevant. Without communication human culture and society could not exist. Beyond this general statement, opinion is divided on the role of mass communication and the role of interpersonal networks. There is a wealth of data in this country (much of it drawn from rural sociology) of studies of the adoption of various farm practices as well as studies of opinion and attitude changes for voting patterns and market research. Two levels of analysis can be identified: a macroscopic level dealing with the effects of mass media upon audiences; and a microscopic level concerned with interpersonal relations among audiences, studies of communications in small groups, and studies of oral communication systems. The latter, drawn primarily from the work of anthropologists, willl be discussed later. In the work of Lazarsfeld, Berelson, and Gaudet (1948), Katz (1957), and others there is a concern with interaction at both levels.

Klapper (1966) has summarized some of the effects of mass communications: (1) media are more likely to reinforce than to convert; (2) media do not typically work directly upon their audiences but function among and through other factors or forces. As we shall see, the general consensus among those concerned with mass media is that the effect of media is rarely direct but proceeds through communication networks.

Rogers (1969) theorizes that communication is the most important variable in modernization among some Columbian peasant villages. His basic hypothesis is that exposure to mass media leads to modernization by creating a favorable attitude toward new ideas. In contrast to Rogers's findings on the importance of mass media, Hockings's (1965) study of communication among the Badaga, Toda, and Kota indicates that it had little effect. He found that although radio provides programs of practical interest, these are never listened to; radio is important only for music.

From these contradictory findings, it seems clear that we cannot postulate a one-to-one relationship between the availability of mass communication and social change (development and modernization). Nor should it be expected that mass communication will have the same importance in all societies. In one it may have great impact, in others, such as the Badaga, almost none.

One of the most valuable theories developed in mass communication research is the "two-step flow" theory developed by Lazarsfeld, Berelson, and Gaudet (1948). According to this theory, some mass media content reaches audiences indirectly through the meditation of "opinion leaders." Opinion leaders are people who are more receptive to mass media, have strong personal influence, and are thus able to pass on information to less active or less receptive sections of the population. Often in the process of passing on information, opinion leaders are expected to evaluate the information. This hypothesis has now been confirmed by other researchers, and it has since been utilized with a large degree of success in the analysis of exposure to mass media and in development programs. The opinion leaders are identified in the desired target group, the message is beamed at them, and the communications networks operate from this point.

Katz (1966) has elaborated the "two-step flow" theory in a recent study of opinion leaders in urban Thailand, whom he calls "key communicators." He introduces the notion of networks, sets of persons who can get in touch with one another, either directly or indirectly. Contacts are individuals who comprise a network. Networks are formed on the basis of linkage among contacts. Identification of key communicators and the kinds of networks and the contacts involved in them provide detailed information on the flow of information in a society. In development programs this knowledge is important to direct the flow of information to different segments of the society.

The work of Stycos (1952) in Greece adds three more categories to the matrix in which communication functions. These are "opinion controller," "opinion and information carrier," and "communications terminant." The opinion controller is distinguished by his ownership of the media. In one Greek village, the tavern owner owned the only radio and could control the programs listened to and the length of time they were heard. An opinion and information leader obtains his information by word-of-mouth and passes it on to others in the community. A communications terminant receives the information and transmission stops with him. Opinion leaders are important in less-developed countries, but status and class barriers may limit their effect.

Communication theory and the theories based on it provide information on the type of communication, its flow, and the networks through which it passes. In some areas of the world, mass communications have been found to be of great importance in change. In other areas they seem to have little effect because of the characteristics of the audience, economic factors, and the matrix in which mass media operate.

Sociolinguistics strives to show the systematic covariance of linguistic structure and social structure, sometimes showing a causal relationship in one direction or the other (Bright 1966:11). Where traditional linguistics has stressed homogenity and treated languages as uniform in their structure, sociolinguistics stresses diversity and attempts to show that variation is conditioned and correlated with specific social differences. Research on bilingualism, multilingualism, and multidialectism are included in sociolinguistics.[2]

An excellent study by Wolff (1959) on intelligibility might be considered a precursor to modern sociolinguistic studies. He found that the criterion of mutual intelligibility between dialects, when measured either by testing the informant or questioning him, did not depend on the linguistic similarity of the dialect, but rather upon social factors and relationships among speakers of different dialects or closely related languages. Further, the relationship between dialects as stated by informants is subject to variation. He cites one example of the Urhobo language, which is spoken in several dialects in the western Niger Delta. One group of dialects, called Okpe-Isoko, is somewhat divergent from the rest of Urhobo, but agreement was general among Okpe informants on high mutual intelligibility between all Urhobo dialects. However, Wolff found that speakers of Isoko claim that their language is different from the rest of Urhobo and that their dialect is not similar enough to the others to serve the needs of normal communication. It turns out that this "vanishing intelligibility" coincides with Isoko demands for political autonomy and ethnic self-sufficiency. The Okpe dialects, almost identical with Isoko, still claim mutual intelligibility with the rest of Urhobo (Wolff 1959:37). Language here serves to reinforce changes in the rest of the social structure.

Fishman, using data available on politically independent polities, has found that a number of differences between linguistically homogeneous and linguistically heterogeneous polities remain even when economic factors are controlled. In the past, linguistic homogeneity has been interpreted as a consequence of other processes such as industrialization, urbanization, modernization, and Westernization (Fishman 1967:24). Fishman's analysis suggests instead that there is a causal relationship at work in the opposite direction. Westernization and development may not be possible for linguistically (and culturally) heterogeneous countries until some degree of linguistic homogeneity is achieved. Studies such as that of Fishman and other studies of bilingual and multilingual societies as well as examination of specific cases of linguistic nationalism may demonstrate that language is one of the prime factors in acceptance or rejection of directed change.

All of the semantic studies considered here examine a portion of the lexicon of specific languages, determine changes in the lexicon, and provide evidence on linguistic acculturation. I do not mean to imply that this is the entire scope of semantic studies, but merely that these are the semantic studies that are most relevant to social change.

With these studies we must again ask whether language and other aspects of culture change differentially, or whether language merely reflects changes in other aspects of culture. For all of the studies dicussed here, language seems to reflect other changes in culture, but we must not assume that this is always the case. Johnson (1943) and Spicer (1943) report that the Yaqui language has been influenced in all its aspects by Spanish. Spicer estimates that nominal loanwords in Yaqui for the categories of domestic utensils, social organization, and ritual are 64 percent Spanish-derived. Contemporary Yaqui culture is a functioning amalgam of Spanish elements and original Yaqui culture. Acculturation was not forced upon the Yaqui, and they freely accepted the culture of the Spanish.

Another situation is reported for the Tanoan languages in New Mexico. For Taos (Trager 1944), Keresan (Spencer 1947), Tewa (Dozier 1964), and Picuris (F. H. Trager 1970) acculturation to lexical items of Spanish or Mexican origin is limited. Loanwords are assimilated to the phonemic structure of the languages, while morphological and syntactic structure are not affected. Dozier (1964: 516) estimates that out of a vocabulary of 2,000 items, less than 5 percent are Spanish in origin. In the presence of Spanish-speakers, loanwords from Spanish are avoided, and loan translations or new formations are made in the native language as a substitute (Dozier 1964:512; F. H. Trager 1970). Dozier attributes the resistence to linguistic acculturation in Tewa to the forceful and coercive nature of early Spanish contact.

Friedrich in his study of changes in the semantic system of Russian kinship terminology from Tsarist to Soviet times attributes all change to economic and social factors. He states, "it is change in social systems that primarily precedes and predetermines change in the corresponding semantic systems" (Friedrich 1966:31). However, he limits this view to the particular case he is describing.

All of the studies mentioned above show language as reflecting other changes in the culture, though none claim that the relationship is always in this direction. More cases of linguistic acculturation must be investigated; then cases may be found that show that the lexicon has changed before other changes in culture.

We turn now to a consideration of those studies dealing with the correlation of a part of a linguistic structure with social structure. We also consider those studies dealing with what has been called "language and culture," that is those studies in which linguistic structure and world view, ethos, and cognitive orientation are considered. These all have their ultimate origin in the von Humboldt-Sapir-Whorf hypothesis. This hypothesis deals with linguistic relativity and states that the structure of language *may* condition our perception and thought. Much time and effort has been spent in proving and disproving this hypothesis. Whorf did not, of course, claim that every bit of linguistic structure is correlated with thought or perception. Because of the intimate and close connection between thought and language, the hypothesis is difficult to test by whatever means. Whorf was never too concerned with the question of whether language patterns or cultural norms came first (Fishman 1966). After a long relationship between a particular language and a culture, Whorf considered that language would be the more rigid, more impervious structure and felt that innovation in culture would have little effect on language. We are not speaking here of surface phenomena, such as changes in the vocabulary, but of the deeper, more pervasive patterns that influence cognition. We can apply Whorf's thought also to the ways in which language is used in various societies and to the differences in social dialects in the same culture and in the same society.

One example of this is Bernstein's (1967) work on *restricted* and *elaborated* codes. A restricted code is speech that uses relatively limited linguistic resources and thus is predictable to a high degree. An elaborated code allows a larger number of structural options and is less predictable. The restricted code is status-oriented rather than person-oriented. It transmits social symbols rather than individual ones. An elaborated code, on the other hand, transmits individual symbols and provides a wide range of meanings from which to select. Speakers of elaborated codes "perceive language as a set of theoretical possibilities for the presentation of . . . discrete experience to others" (Bernstein 1967:129). A restricted code is available to all members of a society, but the lower-class populations have access only to the restricted code, whereas the middle class learns both a restricted and an elaborated code. Bernstein states that this pattern serves both as a reflection and cause of the differences between the lower and middle classes in Britain and serves to maintain them. Unless a child is able to learn an elaborated code, he will remain a member of the lower class, and his development as a member of society will be retarded.

Bernstein's work, while it may have some validity, appears to be an apologia for the class structure of Britain and perhaps an attempt to keep the lower classes in their place. The lower classes also have their elaborated codes and much creativity occurs in the formulation of these elaborated codes, some of which may pass into the code of the middle classes. It is in the interaction between social classes that difficulty occurs. The middle classes will tend to speak a restricted code to the lower classes, who will reply with their own restricted code. Bernstein is saying essentially that if an individual wishes to move out of his social class he must learn to speak the language of the middle classes. If a person from the lower classes intends to succeed in the educational system, he must give up his own language and learn the language of instruction, an elaborated code. Similar statements have been made in America for educating minority-group children, but ongoing research into black English and the learning difficulties of children from other minority groups will hopefully remove this elitist attitude from education. Bernstein would do well to consult some of the American material available on similar situations.

Just as Bernstein shows that different codes may have different effects in the social process, Bright (1967) demonstrates that caste dialects in India have different semantic structures, reflecting different ways of classifying nonlinguistic phenomena. He suggests that these may reflect differences in cognitive orientation from one caste to another (Bright 1967:190).

Detailed studies of semantic systems and other linguistic aspects of a language hold great promise for identifying factors operative in the formation of cognitive maps and patterns of categorization that will aid in determining processes of change.

In the present context the theory of generational stratification will be discussed only in reference to linguistic change, though I hope in the future to apply it to other forms of social change. The hypothesis, briefly stated, says that language has within it the seeds of its own change. Language is constantly changing and evolving; it is not homogeneous, but heterogeneous and nonuniform. This nonuniformity provides the material for change. Change proceeds in all aspects of a language and may be apparent among speakers of a language in generational stages. Change will occur regardless of outside influence but will normally be accelerated by contact with other languages. Although change occurs in phonology, morphology, semology, and semantics, change may occur at different rates in these areas. We are aware of the rapid change in vocabulary among generations, but we have rarely investigated changes in other structural aspects.

Sandia, a Tanoan language spoken in New Mexico, shows changes in phonology, morphology, and semology from the time it was first described (Trager 1939) until the present (Brandt 1970a). Specific information on the changes will not be presented here, but may be found in Brandt (1970a, 1970b). Generational changes in phonology have been found by Boas (1940) for Kwakiutl, Newman (1944) for Yokuts, Samarin (1967) for Badaga, Greenfield (1970) for White Mountain Apache, Leap (1970b) for Isleta, and Bohannan (1970) for Tiv. All of these cases simply report that there is a difference between the speech of various age groups and specify what these differences are. Haugen (1966:42) reports generational differences by decades among speakers of one Norwegian dialect, including some children aged eight to nine who had abandoned "one of the pillars of the dialect, the dative case." It is not possible to say that the language of the children will be the language of the future, because among some groups of speakers a countertendency operates so that children gradually adopt a form of the language spoken by middle-aged people (Haugen 1966:43).

At Sandia no countertendency is evident, but Leap (1970c) has stated that teen-agers as they grow older speak a language closer to that of the middle-aged group. Three generational varieties of Sandia can be distinguished that differ from each other in phonology, where addition, deletion, and rearrangement of the phonological system have taken place. In morphology, subject-object verbal prefixes are so different between the generational varieties of the language as to be almost unrecognizable, and in semology also. This means that each generation of Sandia speaks, in some respects, a different language. This is culture change already accomplished in the language, such that there is a built-in "generation gap" in language. This is particularly important in the semological and semantic system of the language. For it is in these systems that we gain some understanding of how reality is talked about, if not perceived. The "new ethnography" relies heavily on the "native" view of events and processes. Folk taxonomies and paradigms collected by an ethnographer utilize verbally coded material and are linguistic as well as cultural data. Since each variety of Sandia exhibits in all aspects of the language, including semology and semantics, we thus have a testable hypothesis. We can take the linguistic structure for each variety of the language and see how it can be correlated with changes in the rest of the culture, hypothesizing that changes in the language will have ramifications in the culture.

One example of this can be shown for Isleta, a language mutually intelligible with Sandia.[3] The language contains a class of nouns marked by a prefix *na-* which has the semological reference of enclosed space. That is, all nouns possessing a *na-* prefix refer to enclosed space, such as house, *nathô*. Using data from Isleta del Sur, another related language, and early recordings of Isleta, Leap (1970a) has determined that the semological referent for the *na-* class has changed from enclosed space to collectivity. And where the word for house previously referred to an enclosed space for living purposes, it now refers to a collectivity of rooms, sharing the same outside wall. This change in the language can have occurred no earlier than 1885 and no later than 1910. This change has also occurred in the semological and semantic structure for the word for village, *natš a'i*. Originally this referred to a village or pueblo as an area of enclosed space, bounded by a village wall, the area inside the wall being the space in which the ceremonial life of the village took place. With the change in the language, this term still has the semantic reference, village, but now refers not to ceremonial areas at all, but to a settlement which has elected governing officials—the collectivity reference. The notion of a village as a governing collectivity would not have existed before 1885. I think it is clear, then, that changes in the language can have important ramifications for changes in the culture.

We might ask now how these generational changes in language

come about. There are several possibilities. One explanation is based on the process of language acquisition. A child first learns language from his parents or from those caring for him at the earliest stages of life. Thereafter he learns much of his language through interaction with his peer group. When language is transmitted, it is possible that errors of transmission (or "noise" in the communication model) will obscure some of the distinctions. Thus a child learns a slightly different variety of the language from that his parents learned. It is also possible that a child may unconsciously or consciously select from the range of variability present in the language somewhat different features that may later be reinforced by contact with his peer group. This can be illustrated by an example from phonology. The phoneme /i/ in Sandia has an allophonic range of [i I^I e] Some of these allophones may be in free variation, that is, unconditioned variants. In this situation, only one free variant may be favored by the child. A similar process would be operative in other aspects of the language. Language always has a large amount of redundancy, the source of the variability. This choice of one particular feature and its consequent prominence may not affect the language if language is considered abstractly, but it will affect such things as categorization and possibly cognition.

Another possibility for change comes with increasing white contact for Sandias. They are now multilingual, speaking Spanish, English, and Sandia. Where formerly they may have had to control many stylistic variants of Sandia appropriate in different contexts, they now have to control only a few, while English is used in other contexts. Thus they may learn only one style or two. English and Spanish may also have had direct influence on the language through acculturation to English and Spanish linguistic models.

Change in the semological structure and the semantic structure of the language may cause changes in cognitive orientation in the individual. Changes in cognitive orientation may then have some effect on other cultural aspects.

There is some evidence from Isleta and Sandia that change in the language has affected political behavior at Isleta and ceremonial activity at Sandia. This cannot be demonstrated conclusively at the present time, but research is in progress.

Several different approaches to language study have been discussed here. These approaches are (1) communication theory and mass communication, (2) sociolinguistics, (3) linguistic acculturation studies, (4) Sapir-Whorf studies, and (5) generational stratification. Specific studies under these general headings were examined. These studies have demonstrated that we still do not know the exact role of language and communicative behavior in the process of change. Evidence from studies of mass communications and communication networks, such as the two-step theory, show that the effects of media are not direct but pass through networks which differ from society to society. Media tend to reinforce attitudes rather than change them. In some societies change programs that employ radio or television as a vehicle for transmission of information will fail because programs are not listened to. Because different cultures vary with respect to the way in which they respond to mass media we should not expect to be able to develop a cross-cultural theory of the effects of media; but in societies in which change programs operate, studies of the networks that transmit information may be very valuable.

The sociolinguistic approach, in practice, is more specific and therefore less general than the communications approach. As such, it provides more detailed information about links between language behavior and social structure. It provides a better chance for finding correlations or interrelationships between change in language and change in social structure.

Studies of linguistic acculturation are studies of change in one cultural system, language. In connection with studies of semantic change they may provide us with a description of the change process for a particular group.

Studies such as those covered by the term "Sapir-Whorf" or "language and culture" show the most promise for explicating the process of change on the individual level as changes due to difference in cognitive orientation. The theory of generational stratification fits in this category. This area should prove to be significant in the future. A resurgent new interest in problems of language and cognition is already evident. Language is a system just as is kinship, economics, or religion. We have evidence that changes in other systems affect language. We should not readily assume that language does not initiate culture change. The example presented from Isleta is suggestive of a case in which language change has modified other cultural behavior. Increasing research in semantic studies, in particular, and in all areas of language will bring us to a deeper understanding of the process of change.

NOTES

1. I would like to express my gratitude to William Leap and to Raymond Fogelson who read earlier drafts of this paper and provided me with a number of useful criticisms.
2. I do not mean to imply that sociolinguistics concerns itself only with

studies of this type. It is much broader than my statement implies but has
been limited for the purposes of my discussion.
3. I would once again like to express my gratitude to William Leap for
bringing this example to my attention and for giving me permission to use it.

REFERENCES

Bernstein, Basil, 1967. Elaborated and Restricted Codes: An Outline. In
Explorations in Sociolinguistics, Stanley Lieberson, ed. (Bloomington: Indiana
University), pp. 126-133.
Boas, Franz, 1940. Note on Some Recent Changes in the Kwakiutl Language.
International Journal of American Linguistics 7:90-93.
Bohannan, Laura, 1970. Personal communication.
Brandt, Elizabeth A., 1970a. Origin of Linguistic Stratification: The Sandia
Case. *Anthropological Linguistics* 12:36-40.
————, 1970b. Sandia Noun Class Morphology and Semology: A Historical
View. Paper presented at the Sixty-ninth Annual Meeting of the American
Anthropological Association, Nov. 19-22, San Diego.
Bright, William, 1966. The Dimensions of Sociolinguistics. In *Sociolinguistics,*
William Bright, ed. (The Hague: Mouton), pp. 11-15.
————, 1967. Language, Social Stratification, and Cognitive Orientation. In
Explorations in Sociolinguistics, Stanley Lieberson, ed. (Bloomington: Indiana
University), pp. 185-190.
Dozier, Edward P., 1964. Two Examples of Linguistic Acculturation: The Yaqui
of Sonora and Arizona and the Tewa of New Mexico. In *Language in
Culture and Society,* Dell Hymes, ed. (New York: Harper and Row),
pp. 509-520.
Durbin, Mridula A., 1970. The Transformational Model of Linguistics and Its
Implications for an Ethnology of Religion: A Case Study of Jainism. *American
Anthropologist* 72:334-342.
————, 1971. Transformational Models Applied to Musical Analysis: Theoretical
Possibilities. Paper presented at the annual meeting of the Southern Anthro-
pological Society, April 1-3, 1971, Dallas, Texas.
Fishman, Joshua A., 1966. A Systematization of the Whorf Hypothesis. In
Communication and Culture, Alfred G. Smith, ed. (New York: Holt, Rinehart
& Winston), pp. 505-516.
————, 1967. Some Contrasts between Linguistically Homogeneous and Linguis-
tically Heterogeneous Polities. In *Explorations In Sociolinguistics,* Stanley
Lieberson, ed. (Bloomington: Indiana University), pp. 18-30.
Friedrich, Paul, 1966. The Linguistic Reflex of Social Change from Tsarist to
Soviet Russian Kinship. In *Explorations in Sociolinguistics,* Stanley Lieberson,
ed. (Bloomington: Indiana University), pp. 31-57.
Gerbner, George, 1967. Mass Media and Human Communication Theory. In
The Anthropology of Communication, Frank E. X. Dance, ed. (New York:
Holt, Rinehart & Winston).
Greenfield, Philip, 1970. Personal communication.
Haugen, Einar, 1966. Discussion of a paper of Gumperz. In *Sociolinguistics,*
William Bright, ed. (The Hague: Mouton), pp. 43-44.
Hockings, Paul, 1965. *Communication and Cultural Change in an Emergent
Region of South India* (Stanford: Institute of Communication Research).
Johnson, Jean B., 1943. A Clear Case of Linguistic Acculturation. *American
Anthropologist* 45:427-434.
Katz, Elihu, 1957. The Two-Step Flow of Communication: An Up-to-Date
Report on an Hypothesis. *Public Opinion Quarterly* 21:61-78.
Katz, Fred E., 1966. Social Participation and Social Structure. *Social Forces*
45:199-210.

Klapper, Joseph T., 1966. What We Know about the Effects of Mass Communication: The Brink of Hope. In *Communication and Culture*, Alfred G. Smith, ed. (New York: Holt, Rinehart & Winston), pp. 535-551.

Lazarsfeld, Paul, Bernard Berelson, and Hazel Gaudet, 1948. *The People's Choice* (New York: Columbia University Press).

Labov, William, 1967. The Effect of Social Mobility on Linguistic Behavior. In *Explorations in Sociolinguistics*, Stanley Lieberson, ed. (Bloomington: Indiana University), pp. 58-74.

Leap, William L., 1970a. Tiwa Noun Class Semology: A Historical View. *Anthropological Linguistics* 12:38-45.

————, 1970b. The Language of Isleta, New Mexico. Ph.D. diss., Southern Methodist University.

————, 1970c. Personal communication.

Newman, Stanley, 1944. *Yokuts Language of California*. Viking Fund Publications in Anthropology, no. 2 (New York: Wenner-Gren Foundation).

Rogers, Everett M., 1969. *Modernization among Peasants: The Impact of Communications* (New York: Holt, Rinehart & Winston).

Samarin, William J., 1967. *Field Linguistics* (New York: Holt, Rinehart & Winston).

Shannon, Claude E., and Warren Weaver, 1949. *The Mathematical Theory of Communication* (Urbana: University of Illinois Press).

Smith, Alfred G., 1966. *Communication and Culture* (New York: Holt, Rinehart & Winston).

Spicer, Edward H., 1943. Linguistic Aspects of Yaqui Acculturation. *American Anthropologist* 45:410-426.

Stycos, J. M., 1952. Patterns of Communication in a Rural Greek Village. *Public Opinion Quarterly* 16:59-70.

Trager, F. H., 1970. Personal communication.

Trager, George L., 1939. The Phonemes of Sandia. Unpublished manuscript.

————, and Henry Lee Smith, Jr., 1957. *Outline of English Structure* (Washington, D.C.: American Council of Learned Societies).

Wiener, Norbert, 1966. Cybernetics. In *Communication and Culture*, Alfred G. Smith, ed. (New York: Holt, Rinehart & Winston), pp. 25-35.

Wolff, Hans, 1959. Intelligibility and Inter-Ethnic Attitudes. *Anthropological Linguistics* 1:34-41.

Rural Hippie Communes:
An Experiment in Culture Change

BEN J. WALLACE

DURING the 1960s a subculture of nonconformist young people developed a movement which outraged, confused, and, above all, fascinated immense segments of the American public (see Ald 1970; Hedgepeth and Stock 1970; Hopkins 1968; Wolfe 1968; Yablonsky 1968). The followers of this movement, called hippies, sensationally manifested the frustrations of adjusting to a society which they felt to be highly structured, impersonal, and materialistic. This new cultural experience was marked by rebellion against established goals and moral systems, by drug-induced states of consciousness which they believed suggested the possibility of a better life, and, as one veteran of the Haight-Ashbury expressed it, "a search for a meaningful, wholesome relationship with God, Brother, and Self."

This movement has now evolved into a second phase that is in many ways far different from the initial stage which had its focal point in the Haight-Ashbury section of San Francisco. Upon entering the 1970s the hip culture has reached a critical stage in its development. The purpose of this study is to examine one of the alternative life styles of hip culture—the rural commune.

The term *hippie* appears almost daily in many of the major newspapers in North America. In one case, a journalist applies the term to a high school student who has been arrested for possession of marijuana, and in another, to the disciples of Charles Manson. Although the Manson "family" obviously displayed a strikingly different life style from those of most high school students, the press would have us believe that they are out of the same hippie mold. With the demise of the hip mecca of the Haight-Ashbury, the term *hippie* has lost much of its meaning. It has come to be applied to almost anyone who is different from the standard American Judeo-Christian ideal. And, of course, no one can define the all-American boy or girl.

63

The stereotypic hippie is a person, usually young, who has long hair, dresses in Salvation Army issue or outlandish clothing, goes barefoot, seldom bathes, hitchhikes or drives a VW bus, participates in sex orgies, and most importantly, uses dope. Certain individuals, it is true, are heavy drug users. Some persons participate in sex orgies. Many young people go barefoot in the summer and dress in nonconventional clothing. There are even a few persons who possess all the stereotypic characteristics of a hippie, but they are a minority. They are exhibitionists who make good press. There is no hippie—there are only hippies.

The subjects of this paper are generically hippie, but it should be emphasized that as new age hippies they pursue a different life style from the hippies of the 1960s. They are the people of northern New Mexico whose hip life style is nonestablishment but not necessarily antiestablishment. They are participants in what is sometimes called a counterculture (Roszak 1969) but which I interpret as intentional culture. Their culture is different, but it does not necessarily run counter to the establishment. The new age hippies are living an experiment. They are aware that their beliefs are unlike their parents'. They are intentionally developing a life style they believe is better than that which currently exists in North America. Their clothing, housing, philosophy, and religion are, for the most part consciously designed.

There are four overlapping classes of hippie communal establishments in northern New Mexico: families, communal farms, spiritual schools, and free retreats. In addition to the more or less permanent residents in these microcommunities, we shall later see that there are also other types of rural hippies—"lost souls," "gypsy trippers," and "frisbees"—who reside in the area for varying periods of time. Despite the fact that they are all a part of the generalized hippie subculture, their life ways vary considerably.

The family is one of the oldest of the hip communal concepts. Families tend to be oriented to city and business rather than country and farming. They are coeducational, with all adult members ideally sharing economic, social, and political responsibilities. Adults are usually all married to one another; consequently the pairing of sexual partners on a permanent basis is prohibited. A child's parents are all the family, although in actuality the biological mother assumes the greatest share of responsibility for the welfare of her child. It is practically impossible to identify a child's biological father. Families are usually formed by accident—hippies prefer to call this destiny—and, assuming personal compatibility, the group members begin to share in the economic costs of operating the household. With the establishment of a reasonably sound economic base, family members then attempt to attain the ideal goal of oneness—living, working, and sharing in all the benefits and ills of life.

In addition to this organized type of family, the hip culture is characterized by innumerable less structured and amorphous families. The ideal of the family has led to the proliferation of the concept. Almost any small group or band of hippies usually considers itself a family and, more often than not, they are itinerant people.

In the Taos area there is only one structured family, "The Group." The Group consists of about forty persons in residence with an additional twenty persons scattered throughout the United States. Moderately zealous proselytizers, they are organized on the basis of the Knights of the Roundtable and have taken the titles of lords and ladies. The Group believes that the United States will be converted to communal living by the year 2000. They espouse a nineteenth-century utopian world view and argue that individualism is a thing of the past. They preach interpersonal relations, group expression, harmony, love, and economic productivity. Members of The Group support themselves through the operation of a number of businesses in Taos. Theirs is the only relatively large and structured group marriage in the area.

Theoretically, The Group has no leader—all adults share in the work of their business and in the operation of the two houses they occupy. They strive for group harmony, and in order to maintain it they rely heavily on encounter-therapy techniques. For example, if the family feels a person is unusually lazy he is called before his housemates and severely berated. He is made to feel weak and selfish. In his repentance, he is expected to present a confessional. This very persuasive form of demanding conformity serves to reinforce the position of the group and eliminate nonconforming individuals.

A much smaller and less structured type family may be illustrated by a brief discussion of the relationship between John, Mary, Mark, and Benny. John and Mary have been living together for three years. Mark joined them two years ago, and Benny only a year ago. They work as caretakers on a small ranch in southern Colorado but occasionally go to Taos to visit friends. They consider themselves a family even though only John sleeps with Mary and they may not pool their economic resources. They support themselves in a variety of ways: engaging in a small-time trade in marijuana, doing odd jobs, receiving checks from home or just by "moving around." Moving around can be a self-sustaining, if not profitable, endeavor. For example, in 1968 they went to Puerto Rico for several months as guests of a friend—

as Mark said, "with that fat man who was on a sex trip." This type of family, like most hippie groups, shows little concern for the future. Their closest kin are the "lost souls" to be discussed later.

The communal farm is an extension of the concept of a family. But instead of being city-oriented, communal farmers have turned to the rural areas of North America. As one young communitarian expressed it, "We have a focalization for the earth. That's why a lot of hippies go barefoot. We want to feel the soil between our toes."

As in a family, all members of the communal farm share equally in the responsibility of day-to-day living. Both men and women work in the fields, care for the children, cook, wash dishes, sweep the floor, and so forth. Group marriages are not, however, common. Instead, males and females live as couples in their own tents or houses. More often than not there is a common kitchen and dining area for the farm. A child is the responsibility of the commune, but his mother and her current "husband" show the greatest concern for his overall welfare.

The income of a commune—from group work projects, individual projects, or checks from home—usually goes into a common budget. Individuals, however, if they earn a little money or get a check from home, frequently keep some back for their personal use. Sally, a communal farmer of two years, said the purpose of holding some back was "like when having to split or in case the kids need special medicine."

Communal farms do not happen by accident—capital is needed for land and often for general support. The Taos pattern is for one person to purchase from a few to several hundred acres and then invite his friends or family to join him.

In the Taos area there are five reasonably well-established communal farms which have been in operation for over a year. Naked Beaver, Middle Earth, Milky Way, Royal City Company, and Pork Chop Hill. On most communal farms, farming the land productively is an ideal rather than a reality. Furthermore, not all members of the commune participate in farming. Usually only three or four persons have a "focalization" for farming. Others may help with the farm chores, but those with the focalization assume responsibility for buying seeds, reading books on organic farming techniques, and irrigation control. As farmers, communal dwellers are naive. I met only three or four persons who were able to discuss farming reasonably intelligently. There are no self-sufficient communal farms in Taos County. Communal farmers argue, however, that agricultural success is relative and a good yield for the labor expended is unimportant. To them, the major consideration is the experience—the experience of farming and working with nature.

Unlike the Mexican peasant, the poor American dirt farmer, or the American Indian tribes, all of whom hippies tend to emulate, communal farmers can afford the luxury of a poor yield and crop failure. They are not dependent upon their fields for food. All Taos communal farms are subsidized by one or more wealthy benefactors. Estimates vary, but some realtors suggest that close to one million dollars has been invested in Taos County since 1967 by commune supporters. There is no way to determine how many dollars have flowed into the economy from the mothers, brothers, sisters, and uncles of Taos hippies.

A brief description of Middle Earth will provide a preliminary appreciation for the communal farm. Middle Earth, consisting of fifty-three acres, was purchased by a young man from Florida. He had previously lived in Haight-Ashbury. Charles Lovelady, as he will be called here, bought the acreage for twenty-five thousand dollars. In the summer of 1969 there were about thirty-five permanent residents of Middle Earth. They lived in tepees, small wooden huts, and an adobe house, used primarily as a kitchen. They farmed corn, beans, broccoli, cabbage, lettuce, beets, turnips, radishes, and onions on a four-acre plot. They differed from the family described earlier only in that they lived as couples and they tended to place more emphasis on survival, because of the harsh New Mexico winters. Charles, however, supplied most of the income. The Middle Eartheans felt that their way of life was preparing them for the day when the cities would be destroyed and mankind would be forced to the woods. This glorified primitive way of life was, however, short-lived, for a year later the commune had dwindled to ten persons. Charles left and helped start a new commune, although he remained the owner of Middle Earth.

One other type of communal farm, perhaps unique in the annals of hippie history, is the famous Pork Chop Hill, so vividly discussed in the popular press that even the pseudonym used here will give it little anonymity. Pork Chop Hill had its origin in California in early 1967. Starting with only a few people, its numbers grew within the year to around forty persons. The popular press pictured them as bands of wandering minstrels. These bands of "gypsy trippers" were exhibitionists who wore the most outlandish clothing and drove psychedelically painted buses. Their most popularized concept was "hog consciousness." Because of growing resentment from their neighbors in California—probably the event which most upset the locals was the appearance in the press of an American flag above a pig in his sty —the people of Pork Chop Hill were run out of the community. They packed up their belongings, their now famous pig, Pigasus, and in a caravan of five buses moved to the new hippie mecca, New Mexico.

They maintained a home base in New Mexico but continued their gypsy tripping life style, traveling from place to place. In the summer of 1969 they received considerable press from the services they performed at Woodstock and at a Dallas pop festival where they served as a "security please force." It is worth noting that, in general, the press was favorable—the police chief of Lewisville, near Dallas, congratulated them for the excellent job they had done. (The police chief later resigned from his job.)

In October of 1969 the Pork Chop people were to go to California to participate in a seven-day starve-in. Mechanical trouble and weather prevented them from arriving on time, and their whole west coast trip became a fiasco. The band broke into two factions: some stayed with its spiritual leader who asked for nothing, not even Pigasus or their bus, the Road Hog. Others drifted back to the home base in New Mexico. Those that drifted back have started a new communal experience. In the spring of 1970 they numbered about twenty persons and had a house, some goats, chickens, rabbits, cats, and dogs, and a fleet of buses and cars. They started farming.

By tradition the Pork Chop Hill people are "gypsy trippers," itinerants intent on doing their own thing, but they did plan a communal farm. Some of the members are still wandering, and others have settled down for the time being. Pigasus still lives.

There are two spiritual schools in Taos County, one established in the spring of 1967 and the other in January 1970. Both schools are still experimenting with the concept of community but Deva Foundation, the older of the two, has in its short existence created several impressive buildings, which include living quarters, a meditation room, a library, a solar-heated greenhouse, a kitchen, and a barn. Without doubt, Deva is the most visually impressive of the Taos communes. Love, the more recent of the schools, is still in a very early stage of its experiment, and only time will tell the philosophical and physical shape it will take. Both schools are nonprofit corporations and are supported through gifts and donations. Like the communal farms, they are not self-sufficient. Important concepts characterizing Deva and Love are "thy will be done," the refinement of self through prayer, meditation, community service, and creative activity. Neither allows drugs or alcohol on the grounds.

Deva Foundation consists of about fifteen permanent residents. They share equally in the work of maintaining their community, which involves farming, tending chickens and goats, beekeeping, cooking, landscaping, child care, pottery, weaving, maintenance of tools, automobiles, and buildings, and construction. The daily schedule also includes meditation, chanting, religious study, and body movement exercises such as Yoga and Tai Chuan.

Although allowing visitors only on Sundays, Deva encourages people to attend their program of basic studies. Persons may make application to live and study at Deva for a month or more during the summer months. Tuition is a hundred dollars, and room and board is sixty dollars a month. People participating in the program share in the daily work and religious activities of the community. Teachers, such as Zen masters, Sufi dance instructors, and specialists in weaving or in the tea ceremony usually reside there during the summer.

There is no way to convey realistically the message or life style the people at Deva are trying to attain. The success of Deva depends upon the individual point of view. To some, Deva is a heaven on earth, while to others it is a coeducational monastic army with the "top sergeant on a God trip." One of the best means of illustrating at least the ideal is to let people of Deva speak for themselves, as in this selection from one of their brochures.

Who us is gradually becomes clearer. Mostly it is all sorts of people who are willing to come here & try thru all the darkness within & without to find the light & having found it to nurture it & coax it & bless it & wrestle with it & wrestle with it some more & that within them/our self which trys to quench the lite. We do this in order with God's help, that somehow, some way there could be more lite in this world of ours.

Us is a process of becoming fitting together & falling apart. It changes & we change & it changes. And it comes that upon a warm winter day we find our self, just sitting by the side of the barn, together people, animals, sky, trees, earth just us . . . here. On the planet together somehow—someway.

Free, nonstructured retreats are fluid and amorphous hip experiments. Although generally called communes, they are primarily way stations for itinerants. One of the important considerations in the hippie view is that they are a good place to "crash"; wanderers, lost souls, runaway students, and others may stay there for a day or as long as several months. They are a hip hobo heaven. Families, communal farms, and schools discourage (and in many cases prohibit) people from crashing. Free retreat dwellers emphasize freedom, "do your own thing," "this land is God's land," dope, and the love of nature. Free retreaters are as often as not dope freaks. They are also bound together in their opposition to communal farms, schools, and families.

Many of them have lived in these types of hippie establishments for varying periods of time and have had negative experiences. As one young man expressed it, "you get bad vibes in the communes." He went on to note that living in a commune is akin to being in the army or being in jail—"rules, rules, rules, rules."

Three types of people are to be found in the free retreats: "gypsy trippers," "lost souls," and "frisbees." Gypsy trippers (similar to some of the Pork Chop Hill bands) are committed to the hip life but do not choose to live a sedentary life style. Lost souls, also generally committed to hip life, are the hippie individualists—they want to do their own thing. Frisbees—usually teenagers and young college students—flock into Taos during the summer by the hundreds. About all they know of the hip life is what they have read in the newspapers. In Haight-Ashbury they were called "plastic hippies" or "teeny boppers." Perhaps a more appropriate contemporary term would be "summer session heads."

A description of Glory Hallelujah Encampment and some of its residents will serve to illustrate the free retreat life style. Glory Hallelujah Encampment, consisting of eighty-eight acres, is located in a very picturesque but isolated section of the mountains southeast of Taos. The land was purchased in 1969 by a New York physician for his son who had gone to New Mexico to carve for himself a new life style in nature. The physician's son and about ten other persons operate and maintain Glory Hallelujah Encampment. They have erected a few wooden shacks and also do some gardening. But the word is out—Glory Hallelujah Encampment is a good place to crash. In mid-summer 1970 there were about fifty persons in the encampment, mainly lost souls and frisbees.

One of the most striking features of Glory Hallelujah Encampment is the friendliness of its residents. "Hey man—is this a good place to crash?" A young man, sitting in the nude with a bowl of cream of wheat between his legs, replied, "Far out!" "Wow, groovy," was the response of a young girl sitting nearby.

The people of Glory Hallelujah Encampment live a very relaxed life; they eat, drink, work, smoke, and love at their own leisure. Nudity is encouraged as an expression of man's relationship with nature—God's children go naked in the Glory Hallelujah Encampment. Mike, an ex-Colorado draftsman and the man with the cream of wheat, said, "Many people are heavy into God and dope." It should be emphasized that the vibes in Glory Hallelujah Encampment differ greatly from those in communal farms or spiritual schools. Communally established people tend to be generally uptight—worried about themselves and the world. In contrast, the lost souls of Glory Hallelujah Encampment are reminiscent of the flower children of the late 1960s.

Roy and Gail, ages twenty-one and nineteen respectively, made their way to Glory Hallelujah Encampment in a battered station wagon from Berkeley via the riots in Isla Vista in the early summer of 1970 in search of a place to "get their heads together." They thought Glory Hallelujah Encampment would be their place, but after arriving they decided that they preferred life in the city. "It's too hard to get work here," Roy said. "We don't need much, but we have to have food for our four dogs." Gail noted, "We have water and everything we need." Their only income is an occasional check from Gail's mother. Roy and Gail say they have no particular religious or political philosophy. They just wander from place to place, doing their own trip. They plan to return to California for the winter.

Butch is a twenty-one-year-old dropout from a college in Colorado. This is his first experience at living in a communal setting. He has become disillusioned with the American political system and the war, and sees himself as an ex-revolutionary. He does, however, still consider himself a political radical and is very proud of the fact that he participated in riots at the Chicago Democratic National Convention in 1968. His political naiveté is apparent even to some of the other people at Glory Hallelujah Encampment, and his rhetoric is a bore. Butch may go to California, Cuba, or Africa; he may stay at the encampment; or he may return to school. About all he is willing to commit himself to is, "I hate pigs."

Dave is a "Jesus freak." About thirty and a veteran of the U.S. Army, he has wandered from coast to coast. His most recent non–New Mexico communal experience was in a family in Greenwich Village, but as he explained it, "I left because it was becoming a flophouse for freaks." He believes that New Mexico is the last hope for mankind, although he is not convinced that the established communes as they exist today are for the future. "Glory Hallelujah Encampment is God's land." Dave believes that people must return to God through prayer. In fact, prayer is the answer to all his problems. For example, Butch said he needed twenty dollars and Dave suggested that he should pray and ask God for guidance—"God will provide for you." Dave plans to build a house at Glory Hallelujah and live there with Susie, his twenty-two-year-old wife.

Susie is from San Francisco, but most recently she lived at Moon Setting communal farm near Taos. She is outspoken about her dislike for the communal farms. Her bitterness stems from an incident that occurred in the spring of 1970, when her friend Nancy's dog was shot and killed at Moon Setting. She expressed herself as follows: "That son-of-a-bitchin' bastard . . . that owns the place is on a dog killing trip. He's on a God trip. If I could get my hands on him I would cut him. I would stake him out . . . and let the ants eat him. That's what the Indians did, isn't it?" Susie plans to stay at Glory Hallelujah Encampment with Dave and their small child.

As noted, "frisbees" are primarily high school or college youths who know very little about the hip movement. They are out for kicks—usually they are on a dope or sex trip. Except that they serve as carriers of the hip culture when they return home in the fall, they contribute very little to communal life or culture. Hundreds, perhaps thousands, of frisbees come into Taos during the summer. Four days after spring quarter ended at the University of California campuses, I was standing at a stop light in Taos and counted twenty-two cars occupied by "hippie-looking" persons, most of whom were probably frisbees. In the summer of 1969, Middle Earth had fifteen hundred visitors; twelve people spent the winter there. The Haight had its teeny boppers and plastic hippies; the pop-rock groups had their groupies; Taos has its frisbees.

In summary, the following descriptive designations may prove useful when examining communitarian culture in particular, and hip culture in general.

"Aspiring Aquarians" are people who live and aspire to live the family, communal farm, or spiritual school experiment. They believe strongly that they must prepare themselves for the Aquarian or Golden Age. We are in a transition between the Piscean and Aquarian ages. The Aquarians are in transit between Haight-Ashbury and the future. They believe that the new age will be a period of peace, brotherhood, and spiritual growth, but only those persons who have prepared themselves to live in the Golden Age will survive the catastrophes that will precede it. Communal living is the Aquarian preparation.

"Gypsy trippers" are antiestablishmentarians who are not yet convinced that the path to security in the new age rests in sedentary communal living. They are committed to the hip life but still have one foot in Haight-Ashbury and the days of carefree existence. Their lives still revolve around nomadism, entertainment, sex, dope, and psychedelica. These are small unstructured families or bands, both urban and rural oriented, that receive the most attention from the popular press. They differ from lost souls in that they have a historical tradition in the hip movement and tend to be more structured.

"Lost souls" are the "new age" flower children. Some of them are "new" children and some of them are "aging" children. As the name implies, they are wanderers, lost souls—they are hippie hobos. Like the gypsy trippers they emphasize exhibitionism, freedom, sex, and dope. But unlike the gypsy trippers, they tend to be against established communal living. They are still on their own personal trips.

"Frisbees" are the lawyers, businessmen, college professors, physicians, nurses, actors, artists, policemen, housewives, lost souls, gypsy trippers, and Aquarians of the future.

In conclusion, the purpose of this essay has been to describe briefly some of the experiments in culture change presently occurring in northern New Mexico. Specifically, I have tried to show that there is no stereotypic hippie. The hip life style is many different styles. One evening I was at Love, and in response to a comment about hippies one of the women present exclaimed, "I am not a hippie!" The man sitting across from her responded, "Yeh, man, but I'm a hippie." Even those persons who are actively living a hip experiment cannot agree on what to name their life style.

I noted that, to some writers, communal living is one aspect of what has come to be called the counterculture, a poorly defined life style associated with American youth. A youth culture involving an interest in drugs, civil rights, the Vietnam War, problems of alienation, ecology, oriental mysticism, and communitarian experiments does exist, it is true, but considering it to be a counterculture is to be unnecessarily negative. The term *counter* implies opposition to or even hostility toward; it is a negative designation. As an alternative I have suggested that we use the concept of intentional culture because it has the advantage of being neutral, suggesting that youth or commune culture is neither good nor bad.

By intentional culture I mean that the adherents of the culture intend change. This does not suggest that they have control of their future but rather that they attempt to set the direction of their culture. In many respects, the concept of intentional culture complements Gonzales's (1970) use of the concept of neoteric society—societies that have arisen only recently and are absent or very shallow in tradition. The communes of today are neoteric societies—societies that have arisen only recently and whose traditions are very shallow. The communes of today are neoteric microsocieties with an intentional culture. They are socially and culturally articulated with North American society as a whole. They are not like the whole societies with partial cultures as described by Kroeber (1948). In Kroeber's view, the various groups of Negritos in the Philippines, for example, constitute several whole societies because they possess important cohesive kinship and other social organizational principles. These same whole Negrito societies have only a partial culture because they frequently do not possess their own language and much of their general culture is borrowed from their Malay neighbors. In contrast the communes are not whole societies, and although much of their culture is borrowed, it is rapidly being intentionally changed. The communitarians of northern New Mexico borrow concepts from the present and the past, from the East and the West, and intentionally and accidentally synthesize them into what they believe to be a better way of life than that offered by the Establishment.

NOTES

1. This paper is based on research conducted in northern New Mexico through the summer of 1970. For their most able assistance in the project, I would like to express my appreciation to Ashley Marable and Veronica Friel. The research was in part supported by a grant from Southern Methodist University. The persons and places in the paper are real. Most names have been changed, however, to protect identity and privacy.

REFERENCES

Ald, Roy, 1970. *The Youth Communes* (New York: Tower Publications).
Gonzales, Nancie L., 1970. The Neoteric. *Comparative Studies in Society and History* 12:1-31.
Hedgepeth, William, and Dennis Stock, 1970. *The Alternative* (New York: Macmillan).
Hopkins, Jerry, ed., 1968. *The Hippie Papers* (New York: New American Library).
Roszak, Theodore, 1969. *The Making of a Counter Culture* (Garden City: Doubleday).
Wolfe, Burton H., 1968. *The Hippies* (New York: New American Library).
Yablonsky, Lewis, 1968. *The Hippie Trip* (New York: Pegasus).

Psychological Aspects of Reform Movements: Weberian Theory and an Indonesian Case

JAMES L. PEACOCK

THE body of theory that frames this article is derived from the writings of Max Weber (1951, 1958, 1967) and from recent extensions of Weber's notions to Asian societies (Ames 1964; Bellah 1957; Geertz 1959; Kirsch 1967).[1] The thrust of these writings is to delineate processes by which religious symbols and beliefs stimulate modernization by rendering it meaningful and legitimate.

From this general body of theory one may abstract a specific hypothesis central to Weber's work: the hypothesis that Calvinism and similar reformist religions radically restructure the individual's pattern of organizing his life from birth to death. This pattern I shall refer to as the "life arc," following Leighton (1959:24). The Calvinist was driven to systematize and rationalize his life arc into a sustained, planned, single-minded movement toward glorifying God and assuring himself of salvation.

Although this argument is greatly in need of precise definition and documentation, it could contribute powerfully to theory concerning psychocultural aspects of modernization. Unfortunately, this particular argument has not been the focus of the major social scientific and humanistic works aimed at elaborating or testing the Weber thesis. The abovementioned writings on Asia, for example, concentrate on the link between religion and society rather than on the more psychological question of how religion transforms the life arc. The same can be said of the numerous Weberian-inspired studies of European history (see bibliography in Eisenstadt 1964:386-397). Nor does the most comprehensive Weberian-oriented psychological treatise, David C. McClelland's *The Achieving Society*, adequately address the question. Like virtually all American students of "culture and personality," McClelland concentrates on merely the childhood phase of the life arc. Investigating the influence of child-rearing on the achievement motive (McClelland's version of Weber's Protestant Ethic), McClelland says little about the relation between the achievement motive and the patterning of the life arc as a whole. Nor does he adequately explore the relation between the achievement motive and *concepts* of the life arc. McClelland does analyze stories which could reveal such concepts—but only if the structure of their plots were dissected after the fashion of the folklorists (e.g., Dundes 1963) so that one could assess the extent to which a character syste-matizes and rationalizes his life from opening to closing scene. Be-cause McClelland counts frequencies of achievement-related items rather than analyzing structures of achievement-oriented plots, he does not really address Weber's question concerning rationalization of the total life arc.

Studies that do focus on the structure of the life arc, such as that by the psychiatrist Leighton (1959), do not exploit the Weberian notions regarding the role of reformist belief. Concerned not so much with the socioeconomic as with the psychological ramifications of modernization, such psychiatric studies could profit from Weber. In-deed, economic aspects of Weber's thesis can be rejected while still utilizing his insights into the relationship between modernization and psychology.

As Geertz (1959, 1963) and others before him (e.g., Wertheim 1956) have observed, reformist Islam in Indonesia comprises a set of beliefs and is linked to a style of life which strikingly resembles those of Weber's Calvinist-capitalists. Geertz characterizes Javanese members of the devout and reformist Muslim minority (*santri moderen*) as merchants who work hard, live ascetically, and organize themselves in a tightly knit, aggressive, energetic organization for social reform called Muhammadijah.

Strongly contrasting with this santri moderen minority are the majority of Javanese, the *abangan*. The abangan are not active Muslims since they do not attend the mosque, perform the five daily prayers, fast during Ramadan, or desire even slightly to make the pilgrimage to Mecca. The abangan are peasants and proletarians, bureaucrats and aristocrats, but rarely merchants. They relish sensual distractions such as dance, drama, and song. Instead of Muhammadijah, they join the PNI (Indonesian National party) or (before the Gestapu massacre of 1965) the PKI (Indonesian Communist party).

These portraits drawn by Geertz give an impression that the santri compare with the abangan in much the same way that Weber compared reformists in general (exemplified by the early Calvinists) with the traditionalists in general (exemplified by the early Catholics). A closer look reveals that the fit between the Indonesian case and Weber's theory is less neat and more subtle than this. Yet the fit is there. In any event, the aim is not to test the theory by matching it against a case but rather to enrich the theory by examining the myriad colorations which its postulated patterns assume in concrete situations.

What I shall say about the santri moderen derives from a field study of their principal organization, Muhammadijah, which I carried out in Indonesia from January to July 1970. Two classes of data will be presented: first, observation based on the seven months of participant observation of the Muhammadijans; second, a survey of 425 males in the rural and urban areas of Jogjakarta, Central Java, roughly half of whom were Muhammadijah and half of whom were not.

I should mention in advance that indications that a survey respondent *was* Muhammadijah were of three types: cultural, social, and psychological. The cultural questions concerned belief; the social questions, group membership; and the psychological ones, learning experience. Thus respondents were asked to indicate which of several theological positions, including one officially supported by Muhammadijah, they preferred. Respondents were asked to which neighborhoods and organizations, including the Muhammadijah organization and neighborhoods predominantly Muhammadijan, they belonged. Respondents were asked what kind of education, including education in Muhammadijah schools, they had experienced. By and large, the varied indices were similar in the *direction* of prediction. However, they differed in strength of prediction. To belong to Muhammadijah, live in a Muhammadijah neighborhood, or profess a theological position consonant with Muhammadijah most strongly predicts (as measured by chi-square tests) the attitudes and actions relevant to this paper. Muhammadijah schooling, especially after the elementary level, is generally a weaker predictor.

Muhammadijah was founded in 1912 in Jogjakarta by K. H. A. Dahlan. Though Jogjakarta remains its headquarters, it now has roughly six hundred branches in every corner of Indonesia, from New Guinea to Northern Sumatra, and even in non-Muslim areas such as Hindu Bali and Christian Menado. A few branches are found also outside Indonesia, in Singapore and Malaya. Muhammadijah is principally a missionary organization. Its mission is not to convert the heathen, however, but to purify the practices of the nominally Muslim abangan so that they conform perfectly to the principles set forth by

Muhammad in the qur'an and sunnah. Though missionary work (*da'wah*) is primary, an important secondary activity is social and educational reform. Muhammadijah has been more active than any other indigenous Indonesian organization in the building of schools, and it has also built hospitals, orphanages, and the like.

A major target of Muhammadijah's missionary impulse is the Javanese *slametan*, a communal feast believed to harmonize the group with the spirits as conceived largely by Buddhist-Hindu-animist tradition. Muhammadijah believes that because the slametan is not in accord with the qur'an and sunnah, it should not be practiced by true Muslims and that holding the slametan is a waste of time, money, and energy. Elimination of the slametan is one ideal which the Muhammadijans have to an impressive extent achieved in their own lives, as is indicated by personal observation and by the survey statistics that concern the two main sequences of slametans—those that usher in life and death. The life sequence consists of the *tingkeban*, held roughly two months before birth, the *brokohan*, held at birth, and the *selapanan*, held one month after birth. The death sequence consists of the slametans held at 3, 7, 40, 100, 365, and 1,000 days after a relative's death. Whereas few Muhammadijans (roughly 20 percent of the Muhammadijan sample) practice these rituals, a majority of the abangan (roughly 80 percent of the abangan sample) continue to do so.

The cessation of birth and death slametans encourages Muhammadijans to conceptualize and organize the life arc in a new way. Birth and death slametans partially determine an individual's entry into life, the course of his life, and his entry into the next life. To cease the slametans, then, throws responsibility for these matters onto the individual himself.

Muhammadijans believe in heaven and hell, in salvation and damnation in the next life. Rejecting the slametan and (to a certain degree) other ritual determinants of the individual's fate in this life and the next, they consider that salvation or damnation depends on how the individual relates to God. Two modes of relating to God are considered. One is episodic and subjective, the other methodic and objective. The episodic, subjective pattern splits the life arc into disconnected instantaneous and mystical encounters with God which yield conversion, self-transformation, and salvation, as in Pentecostalism and Sufism. Muhammadijans prefer the methodic and objective, where one methodically organizes one's actions as well as thoughts so that they continuously conform to the law of Allah, thereby assuring salvation.

In a short story entitled "Before Long, Perhaps . . . " published in the magazine *Suara Muhammadijah* ("Voice of Muhammadijah"), a young man habitually fishes with an old man who lives a life of pleasure. The old man says he wants to "spend my life from inn to inn." The young man abandons his fishing and organizes his life so that he works at an accounting office in the morning, studies book-keeping in the afternoon, and reads religious books in his spare time. He exclaims, "With my programmes I was no longer lonely. How delightful it is to have a regular life with clear plans and aims. I no longer wished to have a wild friend, the old man included." But one midnight comes a knock at the door. It is the old man, frightened of death. The young man convinces him to accept Allah, join a religious body, and leave all his savings to it three days before he dies. The young man concludes, "Who can be sure when and where death will come to us. The old man, the humorous fatalist, could not escape it. Before long, perhaps, it will come to us—to you readers." The story reveals a concern with methodically organizing the life in its oc-cupational and devotional aspects—rather than living episodically "from inn to inn"—in order to fulfill the commands of Allah and assure salvation. The same concern is reflected perhaps in the fact that a much larger proportion of Muhammadijans than abangan in-dicated on the survey that their thoughts were centered less on a certain nostalgic remembrance than on the desire to "plan my entire life in order that I carry out the law and mission that has been given by God to me." In choosing between the two orientations, the abangan split fifty-fifty, whereas 85 percent of the Muhammadijans chose the "mission" statement and only 15 percent chose the nostalgic statement.

For the Muhammadijan, having a mission in life means doing missionary work (*da'wah*) as part of the struggle (*berdjuang*) in the Muhammadijah organization. Many of the early Muhammadijans, in-cluding the founder, K. H. A. Dahlan, were itinerant merchants, and they became roving missionaries as well. The contemporary Muham-madijans tend increasingly to work as teachers, doctors, and bureau-crats, but the tradition of the roving missionary remains strong. Young Muhammadijans converse enthusiastically about adventures they encounter through traveling from town to town to speak at mosques and religious meetings. Endurance in doing da'wah through one-night stands elicits the same kind of admiring comment from young Muhammadijans that a fullback's power might elicit from young football players. The endurance is said to reflect an ability to *berd-juang dengan ichlas,* to struggle for the cause while maintaining a calm heart.

The following dialogue was between a male instructor and a female student in a so-called mental destruction session which was part of a five-day training camp for female students of the Muhammadijah:

> Teacher: It is IMM (Muhammadijah Student Organization) or HMI (Muslim Student Organization) that most attracts your loyalty?   [The student is a member of both.]
> Student: Muhammadijah.
> Teacher: Because your parents are Muhammadijah?
> Student: Muhammadijah better fits my personality.
> Teacher: Why do you struggle?
> Student: To seek experience.
> Teacher: Wrong! You are wasting time! Training merely to seek experience! Do you not understand the meaning of struggle?

The dialogue suggests the extent to which the notion of "struggle" is made explicit within the organizational context of Muhammadijah.

The term for struggle, *berdjuang*, overlaps with the Muslim term, *djihad*, which is often translated as "holy war" but is used by Muhammadijans to refer to virtually any spiritually motivated struggle. Indeed, Muhammadijans share the general Indonesian tendency to speak of symbolic struggle in the same militaristic way Westerners speak of physical combat. Thus at a two-week training camp for male Muhammadijah leaders from Central Java, *berdjuang* was used to refer to military service for Hizbullah (a Muslim militia), to preaching against heretical mystical sects, exterminating Communists, and propagandizing against Christianity. These usages appeared not only in lectures, such as those relating the history of Muslim struggle against Christianity, but also in autobiographies which trainees were required to narrate to the group. The training center itself had a military atmosphere, as in its 6 A.M. sessions of physical conditioning.

Muhammadijans speak of loving (*tjinta*) the organization. They make clear that their love is not sexual or mystical (as in Sufism) but an obedience (*ta'at*) resulting in sacrifice (*korban*). For the rank and file Muhammadijan, struggle within the organization is less a fiery and relentlessly innovative drive than a calm and pious obedience. Much is made of the goals (*tjita-tjita*) of Muhammadijah, but aside from the goals and achievements, the organizational charts and organizational meetings are cherished for their own sake. Muhammadijans compose elaborate agendas (*atjara*) and then introduce one after another speaker saying, "Now Brother X will fill up time (*mengisi waktu*)." Goals are forgotten as members become absorbed in the ritual of meetings.

Some Muhammadijans hold that by continuous conformity to the laws and rites of the qur'an through which the primeval society of Muhammad is recreated, the ills of Indonesia will mysteriously and automatically be cured. Such an ideology would seem to encourage a ritualism of the type perhaps reflected in the Jogja survey. A much larger proportion of the Muhammadijan (85 percent) than abangan (5 percent) respondents to the survey chose to condemn drinking as absolutely taboo rather than to evaluate it functionally. Other evidence could be mustered to suggest that the vaunted Weberian *Zweckrationalität*, the rational evaluation of each plan and action according to the efficiency of its contribution to some specific end, is less prominent in Muhammadijah than in Weber's idealized Calvinism. The rationalism tends to be replaced by a ritualism, a blind obedience to religious law.

In the twenties, Muhammadijah made significant innovations in the education of Indonesian Muslims. It introduced such Western patterns as the progressive series of grades (first, second, etc.) and secular subjects. Yet it has continued to educate more for morality than for creativity. Whether discussing kindergarten or secondary school, the leaders of Muhammadijah education are unanimous in seeing as the major virtue of their system its inculcating of a religious ethic that prevents promiscuous relations between the sexes. None of the leaders spontaneously says anything about schools as places to develop thought, nor do Muhammadijah schools seem designed to encourage such development. Muhammadijah kindergartens have neither building blocks nor drawing equipment, nor have they developed any Javanese equivalents. The chant-and-memorize (*hafal*) method of rote learning throughout the Malayo-Indonesian area is prominent in Muhammadijah schools from kindergarten to college.

Because a Muhammadijan becomes righteous not through an episode of conversion or revelation but through systematic study, his amount of knowledge identifies his amount of righteousness. Early schooling in religion is considered important. Biographies of famous Muhammadijans cite their religious teachers, books, and courses they have taken from childhood on. Muhammadijah religious schooling continues until death, thus differing from the secular governmental school pursued by the abangan; the secular schooling begins with the elementary grades and stops at whatever point the student acquires a government job. Muhammadijah religious schooling is aimed less at any immediate goal than at maintaining throughout the entire life cycle a commitment to the moral principles of Islam.

Muhammad is the prophet of the Muhammadijans, and their leaders exhort them to emulate Muhammad's life. To inquire as to what influence Muhammad's life might have on the life arcs of the faithful, each respondent in the Jogja survey was asked if he could recall any event in Muhammad's life which had made a strong impression on him when he was young. As might be expected, more Muhammadijans than abangan recalled an event. Among those who recalled an event, Muhammadijans were more inclined than abangan to recall Muhammad's wars and struggles, which agrees with their emphasis on *berdjuang*. Muhammadijans split fifty-fifty recalling wars and struggles as opposed to the miraculous ascent of Muhammad to heaven, whereas abangan recalled the miracle 100 percent and wars and struggle 0 percent.[3]

Striking is the extent to which Muhammadijans chose to recall not an event in Muhammad's life (55 percent) but a moral virtue he represented or professed (45 percent); almost as many recalled a virtue as an event, even though they were asked and even pressed to recall an event (*peristiwa.*). Striking also is the small number of Muhammadijans (1 percent) who recalled Muhammad's birth or death. These facts suggest that the Muhammadijan's view of Muhammad differs from the Christian's view of Christ. The law which Muhammed taught is more significant to Muhammadijans than the drama of his life. The reverse is true of Christ, who said, "I *am* the law." Christians commemorate Christ's birth, death, and resurrection, for these compose a drama resulting in mystical salvation. Mukti Ali, a Muhammadijan teacher, displayed keen insight when, at a training center, he exhorted Muhammadijans to compare the holy qur'an not with the Bible but with Christ on the grounds that the qur'an and Christ are the root sources of the Muslim and Christian faiths.

Few of the faithful strive to emulate directly the lives of either Muhammad or Christ, but some parallels may be noted. Christ was born a carpenter, never married, was pacifistic, ascetic, and individualistic. He died young on the cross. Muhammad became a merchant, waged war, married polygynously, headed a community, and lived until old age. Muhammadijan figures such as K. H. A. Dahlan or Hadji Rasul were merchants who to some extent glorified war and struggle, married polygynously, headed communities and organizations, and lived until old age. Muhammadijans feel that the celibacy, pacifism, and individualism of Christ are foreign to human nature, as perhaps they are.

Modern Muhammadijans are usually monogamous. The very Muhammadijan biographies which on the inside display photographs of the Muhammadijan founders with their several wives have on their covers sunshine, a mosque, and a modern Muhammadijah hospital in a street populated by a family of husband, wife, one daughter, and one son. That Muhammadijans harbor monogamous sentiments as well as structure is suggested by the survey, which shows that Muhammadijans cite "wife" as the "person sought to escape from loneliness" twice as often as they cite "parent" or "friend." The trainee at a training center would frequently mention in his autobiography how he and his wife struggled together in Muhammadijah, to which the group would respond sympathetically with such a comment as, "Because you are encouraged by your wife you can truly struggle until you are tired, then quickly sleep."

The picture of the bourgeois family is tempered by statistics showing that Muhammadijan marriages are as often by arrangement as by romantic choice and that twice as many Muhammadijan households are matrilocal or patrilocal as neolocal. Probably the Muhammadijans divorce less frequently than the abangan (whose divorce rate is over 50 percent). The Muhammadijans are circumcised earlier than the abangan (50 percent at age nine or before as opposed to the abangan's 95 percent at 10 or over) but tend to be later in leaving home, going to work, and marrying. All of this suggests a stable if not stifling Muhammadijan arc of domestic life. The Muhammadijan is fed through early circumcision into a lifelong system of study and worship in which he is married to a pious girl chosen by his parents, incorporated into his or her parents' house and possibly their home textile industry, and engaged with his wife in the cozy ritual, ideological, and organizational "struggle" for Muhammadijah until he dies.

The abangan is probably more likely to enjoy a premarital sexual affair than the Muhammadijan, which may partially explain why virtually all abangan whom I asked to narrate their life histories spontaneously told of youthful romance that outshone adult domesticity, whereas no Muhammadijans did. The Muhammadijan quickly shifted into description of his life mission. The difference may reflect values as well as experience, suggesting an abangan tendency toward nostalgia, a Muhammadijah tendency toward militancy. Nostalgia contrasts a current reality with a past pleasure, militancy a current reality with a future ideal.

One difference between early and contemporary Muhammadijans is that the early ones were more likely to embark on the pilgrimage to Mecca in adolescence, while the contemporary ones wait until old age. Most of the early founders of the reformist Islam in the Malayo-Indonesian region brought their ideas back from their youthful pilgrimage to the Near East where they studied.[4] Absorbing modernist ideas while inflamed by youth and adventure, the Muhammadijans came home fiery reformers. Today the Near Eastern doctrines are old fashioned, the pilgrimage is made in old age, and the new generation lacks the fire of the reformer of old.

Through rationalizing his life arc, the Muhammadijan has possibly changed his disposition to mental disease. Scattered data suggest that abangan are more likely than the Muhammadijan to suffer from the disease known as *latah*, whose sufferers compulsively imitate the sounds and actions of others. A striking number of the latah are employed as servants, and many of the latah actions ridicule and exaggerate manners and status of the elite (H. Geertz 1968; see also Peacock 1968: 159, 242) Possibly because the bourgeois Muhammadijans avoid employment in menial posts, possibly because they are concerned with manners and status less than are most Javanese, and possibly because they seem less frequently to utilize the type of Javanese childrearing known as *tuturi*, where a child learns by imitating, Muhammadijans are less prone to latah. On the other hand, one may speculate that the greater Muhammadijan propensity to elaborate schemes, to discover scapegoats, and to feel guilty renders them more vulnerable than the abangan to paranoid and depressive reactions.[4]

The apparent low incidence of latah among the Muhammadijans is associated with a low incidence of dance which in contrast is as highly developed among the abangan Javanese as anywhere in the world.[5] The dance and dance-dramas such as *srimpi, ketoprak, wajang wong*, and *ludruk* are hardly part of the Muhammadijan life. Nor are Muhammadijah children permitted much indulgence in the rich lore of myths and tales that flow from these productions. Their diet is restricted largely to moralistic stories of Islam. Because art threatens to tempt the believer from the straight and narrow path, it is suspect, and beyond defining what is forbidden, Muhammadijah has concerned itself little with the development of art.

Surveying the customs of the Muhammadijans, one can see much which conforms to Weber's Protestant Ethic type. Like the Calvinists, Muhammadijans regard life as a mission. Avoiding the distractions of sex and art, they stick to the straight and narrow. They are monogamous and bourgeois in their conjugality. They are middle-class merchants. They cleanse the world of rites and magic. They distrust mysticism. Though lacking a savior, they have a prophet, whereas the abangan have neither. Compared with the abangan they are militant rather than nostalgic, moralistic rather than poetic. Most important, the Muhammadijans strive mightily to rationalize and organize the life arc.[7]

Yet much of Muhammadijan life is placid. Muhammadijans may cite the Dutch proverb that "time is money," but they also organize meetings and speeches merely to "fill time." They may introduce modern subjects into the Muslim curriculum, but they orient their schools toward a traditionalistic moral control. They may dominate the indigenous Indonesian middle class, but they remain largely at the level of cottage industry and small trade. Muhammadijah as a *movement* may sustain an organized struggle, but the life arc of its typical contemporary *member* tends to run in a pious, cozy, uninnovative rut.

Cultural explanations can be cited for Muhammadijah's deviation from Weber's ideal type. Unlike the Calvinist, the Muhammadijan does not believe he is born a sinner. Hence he does not suffer from the sinner's compulsion to prove that he is of the elect by purifying and rationalizing his life in the most radical and relentless fashion. Believing that he is born good, the Muhammadijan need merely conform consistently throughout his life to the law of Allah, thereby assuring himself that he is ready for death.

Social explanations can also be cited. Traditional Javanese society, especially the nobility, opposed at every level the Calvinistic-type rationalization of life, and that society, especially the nobility, was bolstered by the Dutch colonial government. The Chinese dominated the economy, smothering the true florescence of an indigenous business class. And Muhammadijah's historical period differed from the period of the heyday of Calvinism. Emerging before the rise of communism, socialism, and nationalism, the Protestant Reformation could seize a starring role in the modernization process. Muhammadijah, however, was founded in 1912, the same year that nationalistic movements began to gather momentum in Indonesia, soon to be followed by communism. Resources, and talent that in an earlier era might have gone into Muhammadijah were channeled instead into nationalism and communism as they seized the initiative in the modernization of Indonesia. In fact, these movements compete directly with Muhammadijah since they favor secularism and collectivism rather than the Islamic private enterprise style of life that is championed by Muhammadijah.

In spite of the sociocultural obstacles, Muhammadijah does display many of the tendencies which the logic of Weberian theory would predict. Several tendencies that appear in the Muhammadijah case might be investigated in other cases as well. Thus we might ask whether other reform movements tend to encourage delusional and depressive rather than hysterical mental disorders; whether reform movements necessarily replace comic and tragic patterns of life arc structure with pious and rational patterns; whether, as a general rule, membership in the reformist group and allegiance to its ideology influence the life arc more than does education in reformist schools alone.

Such questions seem to me important for the study of development and change. We have considered the role of politics and economics, family and community, attitudes and motives, but I know of no study that has fully confronted the relationship between modernization and the total life arc of the individual. Weber's work points to reform movements as a major source in transforming the total life arc. The exploration of this hypothesis through comparative study of movements such as Muhammadijah should yield insight into the psychological dimensions of change.

NOTES

1. I wish to express my gratitude to David M. Johnson who performed computer calculations on which this article's statistics are based, and to Charles Hudson and Frank Manning who contributed helpful comments. I am grateful also to the National Science Foundation, the American Council of Learned Societies, and the University of North Carolina, which financed field research and postfield analysis.

2. The percentages cited in this article are based on a sample varying in size according to the particular variables being considered but averaging approximately 200 Muhammadijans and 175 abangan, except where noted otherwise. Other respondents in the sample of 425 were primarily non-Muhammadijan santri.

3. Because few abangan reported recalling an event from Muhammad's life, this comparison is based on an abangan sample of only nine respondents.

4. See the classic biography of Hadji Rasul, Hamka's *Ajahku;* also, Junus Salam, *K. H. A. Dahlan: Amal dan Perdjoangan.*

5. See Opler (1967:69) and Yap (1965) on the low frequency of these symptoms among Javanese in general. However, I have found several cases of contemporary santri moderen who are under psychiatric treatment for depression associated with their feeling sinful. I have found no cases of abangan exhibiting these symptoms.

6. On the relations between latah and Javanese dance, see Peacock (1968:159, 242).

7. I do not claim a causal relationship between joining Muhammadijah and organizing the life arc. Comparison of the individual member's life before and after joining Muhammadijah is difficult because many Muhammadijans were raised from birth in the Muhammadijan context. One case that is amenable to the before/after analysis is that of Muhammadijah's most vocal anti-Christian propagandist who, before he converted to Muhammadijah as a teen-ager, was a Catholic abangan. By a lucky coincidence, in 1953 Prof. Hildred Geertz administered the Thematic Apperception Test to this individual and his family when he was still a Catholic. With this person's permission, I may undertake a comparison between the 1953 TAT records and certain 1970 materials to uncover differences in his attitudes before and after joining Muhammadijah. A second type of before/after analysis that is feasible is historical—comparing typical

Muslim life cycles before and after the date of Muhammadijah's founding in regions where Muhammadijah flourished and failed to flourish. A useful comparison of this type could possibly be made between Central and East Java.

REFERENCES

Ames, Michael M., 1964. Religion, Politics, and Economic Development in Ceylon. *1964 Proceedings of the American Ethnological Society* (Seattle: University of Washington Press).

Bellah, Robert N., 1957. *Tokugawa Religion* (Glencoe, Ill.: Free Press).

Dundes, Alan, 1963. Structural Typology in North American Indian Folktales. *Southwestern Journal of Anthropology* 19:121-130.

Eisenstadt, S. N., 1968. *The Protestant Ethic and Modernization* (New York: Basic Books).

Geertz, Clifford, 1959. *Religion of Java* (New York: Free Press).

——, 1963. *Peddlers and Princes* (Chicago: University of Chicago Press).

Geertz, Hildred, 1963. Indonesian Cultures and Communities. In *Indonesia*, Ruth T. McVey, ed. (New Haven: Human Relations Area File Press).

——, 1968. Latah in Java: A Theoretical Paradox. *Indonesia* 5:93-104.

Hamka, 1957. *Ajahku* (My Father). (Djakarta: Djajamurni).

Kirsch, A. Thomas, 1967. Thai Buddhist Syncretism. Ph.D. diss., Harvard University.

Leighton, Alexander H., 1959. *My Name is Legion.* The Stirling County Study of Psychiatric Disorder and Sociocultural Environment, vol. 1 (New York: Basic Books).

McClelland, David C., 1967. *The Achieving Society* (New York: Free Press).

Opler, Marvin K., 1967. *Culture and Social Psychiatry* (New York: Atherton).

Peacock, James L., 1968. *Rites of Modernization* (Chicago: University of Chicago Press).

Salam, Junus, 1968. *K. H. A. Dahlan: Amal dan Perdjoangan* (K. H. A. Dahlan: Action and Struggle) (Djakarta: Muhammadijah).

Weber, Max, 1951. *Religion of China* (Glencoe, Ill.: Free Press).

——, 1958. *The Protestant Ethic and the Spirit of Capitalism* (New York: Scribner's).

——, 1967. *Sociology of Religion* (Boston: Beacon).

Wertheim, W. F., 1956. *Indonesian Society in Transition* (Bandung, Indonesia: Sumer Bandung).

Yap, P. M., 1965. Phenomenology of Affective Disorder in Chinese and Other Cultures. In *Transcultural Psychiatry*, A. V. S. De Reuck and Ruth Porter, eds. (Boston: Little, Brown).

Evolution and Consequences of a Technological Change Program in Rural Mississippi

JOHN H. PETERSON, JR.

THE rapid change in the nature of American agriculture and the transformation of rural life in the United States has been so generally recognized as to need little discussion. Alterations that are taking place in rural society in the United States include an increase in agricultural productivity through larger commercial farming operations, an increasing number of rural residents engaged in nonfarming operations, a decline in rural-urban differences, and changes in rural social organization in the direction of a decline in primary relationships and an increase in importance of secondary relationships. Yet in spite of the significance of these and other alterations in rural society, there do remain certain "basic persistencies and stabilities" in rural society (Larson and Rogers 1964:60). Any technological change program, therefore, could be expected to be affected by the interaction of the basic stabilities in rural society and the forces which are dramatically altering that society.

This interaction will be examined here in terms of a single technological innovation, rural water systems. The data for this paper were collected through an extensive study of the status of development of rural water systems in Mississippi and an intensive study of rural neighborhoods and water systems in a selected Mississippi county.[1] I will first indicate the nature of rural water systems and forces which operated to limit the initial scope of these systems; next I will examine changes in the scope of organization of rural water systems; and finally I will discuss the impact of rural water systems on rural society.

The vast majority of Americans take for granted an adequate and safe supply of water piped into their homes. Public water

88

systems in urban areas have been so generally accepted that most people take the availability of water for granted except perhaps to complain about increases in their water bills. Yet this is far from the case in the smaller towns and open countryside of rural America, where citizens have only within this decade begun to turn from private wells to community water systems. The United States Department of Agriculture estimates that in 1963, 62 percent of almost thirty-five thousand communities in the United States with populations under one thousand did not have public water systems (Report of the Secretary of Agriculture 1968:60). In open-country rural neighborhoods, public water systems were almost nonexistent.

Rural residents, therefore, have not been able to take their water supply for granted; in fact, they have been facing increasing water problems in recent years. Urbanization, industrialization, and commercial farming operations are extracting increasing amounts of water, resulting in a lowering of the local water table even in predominantly rural areas. The site selected for intensive study clearly illustrates this problem. Mississippi County is similar to the majority of counties of Mississippi, lying not in the delta or coastal areas of Mississippi but rather in the larger hinterland in which small independent farmers predominated until recently. The rural population declined from 70 percent in 1950 to 51 percent in 1970. During the same period, numerous industries were attracted to the area and increasing numbers of rural residents began working in local factories. The nonfarming rural population increased from 19 percent in 1950 to 36 percent in 1970. At the same time, the urban population increased from 30 percent to 49 percent of the total population.

The water table, as measured at the largest urban center in the county, had declined only fifty feet between 1900 and 1950. But the increasing demands for water by local industries and the urban population resulted in a decline of a hundred feet in the water table between 1950 and 1970. The decline in water level was not drastic in rural areas distant from the county seat, but throughout the entire area the water level was beginning to decline rapidly.

As a result, most rural residents were facing the necessity of deepening their wells in order to have a reliable supply of water. This was not a matter of simply increasing the well depth, but usually required reboring the entire well and installing a larger and more expensive pump capable of bringing up water from greater depths. Throughout Mississippi County, rural residents were aware of a water problem. If they had not had problems with their own wells, they knew of neighbors whose wells were going dry. They knew the age and depth of their neighbors' wells and of their own. From a knowledge of their neighbors' expenses, they knew that within a certain number of years they would face a similar expense in re-boring their own wells.

Rural residents were also aware of the impact of the increasing cost of wells on rural building costs. Anyone planning to build a new home in a rural area had to consider in his construction costs between $1,500 and $3,000 for a well. For rural residents no longer engaged in farming, the possibility of building a new home in an urban area served by a public water system was increasingly attractive. While well costs were not the only factor encouraging out-migration from rural areas, older rural residents believed that it was a major contributing factor. In the case of poorer rural residents, well costs alone could constitute a deciding factor in out-migration. Many people simply could not afford the cost of a new well and were forced to haul water from neighbors' wells during dry seasons. The only alternative for them was to leave the rural area and secure housing in nearby towns.

The solution to the increasing cost of private rural wells was seen in community water systems serving all the residents of a given rural area. As a result, new federal legislation was enacted during the early 1960s providing assistance to rural residents seeking community water facilities. A program was established that is in many respects similar to the Rural Electrification Administration established under the New Deal to bring electricity to rural areas. Individuals interested in establishing a rural water system may organize their neighbors into a nonprofit cooperative, in which all members agree to use water from the cooperative water system. Engineers survey the area to determine the tentative location of water lines, the size of the well and tank needed to serve the area, and the cost of constructing the system. Potential cost is compared with the number of potential users to determine if the system could pay for itself within a forty-year period without unrealistically high water rates. If so, potential users apply for a charter as a nonprofit organization, have construction plans prepared, and apply for a loan to cover the cost of establishing the system.

The agency selected to administer this program was the Farmers Home Administration. The FHA was created in 1946 through the merger of the two major credit agencies of the Department of Agriculture: the Farm Security Administration and the Farm Credit Administration. While the emphasis in farm credit programs has varied at times, the FHA and its parent organizations have almost forty years of experience in administering a variety of farm credit programs to meet the changing needs of rural residents (USDA 1963: 212-218, 347). For this reason, the FHA was the logical choice as the agency to administer a program in rural water systems.

As the primary credit agency in the Department of Agriculture, the FHA has loan specialists in approximately seventeen hundred county offices. Through these local FHA supervisors, the FHA was already assisting rural residents in securing low-interest insured loans for farm operations, farm purchase or enlargement, and rural housing. In conjunction with these loans the FHA was active in providing management services to farmers. Although the primary focus of the FHA and its parent organizations has always been the individual rural resident, other loan programs for watershed improvement and community recreation facilities have been administered by the FHA in recent years. Finally, the parent organization of the FHA, the Farm Security Administration, administered a small water system program during the 1930s.

The selection of the FHA as the agency for administering water system loans had major consequences, especially in the early stages of the program. County FHA supervisors were primarily trained and experienced in working with individual rural residents through the already extensive farm and home loan programs. The water system program was simply added to the responsibilities of the local FHA supervisor. Lacking experience in working with community groups and working initially without additional staff and with few guidelines, local FHA supervisors discovered that processing rural water loan applications was a very time-consuming and frustrating task, competing with the necessary supervision they needed to give the more extensive programs of farm and home loans.

Under these circumstances, it is not surprising that some local supervisors were less than enthusiastic promoters of the water system program. In one county, a rural neighborhood attempted unsuccessfully for two years to have a loan request sent to the state FHA office for consideration. After a lengthy initial wait, they were informed that the initial file had been "lost" in the local office and that the file had to be prepared again. For over a year the FHA supervisor could not find time to prepare the loan file. Only after a new FHA supervisor was appointed was a water system loan made in this county.

This was an atypical case, but even when the local FHA supervisor was an enthusiastic supporter of the water system program he operated under certain legal restraints. By law the FHA is allowed to make loans only to individuals and groups unable to obtain credit elsewhere. Essentially, local supervisors are not allowed to solicit applications for loans. This creates little handicap when dealing with individual farm loans, but it did create a problem in the organization of rural residents interested in securing a water system loan. The local FHA supervisor could not go out and organize a group of individuals to participate in a rural water system. Rather he was limited to furnishing information and advice to interested groups and assisting these groups in securing loans after the group was organized and found that they could not secure funds elsewhere. As a result, the role of the local FHA agent in the initial organization of rural water systems was limited by commitment to existing agency programs emphasizing individual rural residents, lack of experience in working with community groups, and legal restrictions.

In most counties, however, there was an active change agent in the form of persons qualified to perform the engineering service necessary for the construction of rural water systems. The authorized cost of rural water systems allowed up to 7 percent of construction costs to be paid for engineering services. In many areas, individuals or companies with engineering skills became active in promoting construction of rural water systems in order to secure business for themselves. In most communities engineering personnel had initial contact with rural leaders at the same time or even prior to contact with FHA representatives. For example, this process took place in one rural neighborhood when a local leader, facing the necessity of constructing a new well, approached several neighbors about digging a common well and sharing the construction costs. He also discussed this with a local well-digger. A representative of a local engineering company heard about his interest and came by to discuss the rural water system program. He suggested that the farmer contact the local FHA supervisor and volunteered to take a preliminary survey of the neighborhood to see if a system was feasible. As a result, he later received the engineering contract to design the water system.

Although engineers could thus at times be more active than FHA supervisors in promoting interest in rural water systems, they also operated under certain constraints. The most important of these was the provision that they would not receive full payment for services until after the system was completed and in service. If they completed a preliminary survey and designed the system but for some reason the local group could not get sufficient members to support the system, the engineer received no compensation for his services.

For this reason, engineers made initial contacts and offered their services to rural neighborhoods which showed the greatest promise of being able to organize themselves quickly and secure a loan.

Because of the restricted roles of the two agents, the FHA supervisor and the engineer, local leadership in rural areas was a major factor in the initial organization of rural water systems. In spite of the changes that are occurring in rural areas, the rural neighborhood still remains an identifiable unit of participation and interaction. Freeman and Mayo (1957:319) have observed that small open-country communities marked by neighborliness and diffuse personal and institutional roles have a relatively clear pattern of leadership dealing with all community issues. In Mississippi County, leadership beyond the individual rural neighborhood seems to operate on a county level. Initially, countywide leaders did not play an active role in water system organization, leaving the organization of rural water systems to leaders who operated primarily in individual rural neighborhoods. This is clearly indicated in the data from Mississippi County. Preliminary research for an earlier study had identified fifty-six individual rural neighborhoods in Mississippi County.[2] Neighborhood identification and boundaries were verified by a panel of county leaders. These leaders were further asked to rate the entire list of neighborhoods in terms of strength of local leadership and degree of participation in local programs. Comparison of this information with information gathered on rural water systems revealed a high degree of correlation between neighborhood boundaries and water system boundaries and between rated neighborhood leadership and ability to organize a rural water system.

In Mississippi County, a total of seven rural water systems were organized and constructed between 1966 and 1970. One additional system is in the process of being funded and three additional systems have accomplished initial organization but have no immediate prospects for funding because of curtailment of funds. Of the seven completed water systems, the first three systems completed lie entirely within the identified boundaries of a single rural neighborhood and serve the vast majority of residents within that neighborhood. The first three systems organized also rank within the top ten rural neighborhoods in the rating of local leadership and two of the three communities rank first and third, respectively. These data, plus interviews with leaders in individual rural neighborhoods, indicate that initially organized water systems in Mississippi County served individual rural neighborhoods with a relatively high level of informal local leadership.

Although water systems could easily be organized on the basis of individual rural neighborhoods, certain disadvantages soon became apparent in this form of organization. In the first place, the processing of a loan application required the same amount of work regardless of the size of the water system being planned. In the early stages of development of the water system program, before detailed guidelines were prepared, processing of loan applications required the investment of a great deal of time by the local FHA supervisor. After the system was constructed, the local supervisor had to devote further time advising each water system until the directors of the system became skilled in its management. The organization of larger systems required less loan processing and supervision.

Second, as the first systems began operating, the inefficiencies of small-scale operation became apparent. Having less financial reserve, the smaller systems were more likely to suffer a major financial blow in the event of equipment failure, and having a smaller number of members they were less likely to have a pool of leadership experienced in the operation of what was essentially a business enterprise, at least in its economic aspects. Smaller systems therefore required a disproportionate amount of supervisory time. Finally, the organization of individual neighborhood systems often conflicted with orderly development of water systems for a larger area. Many smaller neighborhoods were not large enough to permit construction of an individual system, but they could be served by a common system shared with one or more other neighborhoods. Construction of systems serving only larger neighborhoods without regard for smaller adjacent neighborhoods would leave these smaller neighborhoods permanently dependent on individual wells.

As a result, local FHA supervisors began early in the program discouraging the formation of additional small single neighborhood water systems. Where a neighborhood interested in securing a water system was adjacent to a neighborhood already having a system, they encouraged a supplemental loan to the established system enabling it to extend its service to the unserved neighborhood. When a neighborhood was not adjacent to an established system, they encouraged this neighborhood to join with adjacent neighborhoods in organizing a single large water system.

In spite of this shifting emphasis, single neighborhood systems continued to be constructed, especially where joining another system was not feasible because of the design and location of surrounding water systems. Organization of systems serving more than a single rural neighborhood was most readily accepted when the individual rural neighborhoods were not of sufficient size to permit construction of a water system. However, it is important to note that the unit of organization usually continued to be the individual rural neighborhood. Of the four water systems in Mississippi County serving members outside a single neighborhood, a single rural neighborhood formed the center of the system to be organized, and the leadership in that neighborhood took the major initial steps in organizing the system. In one system, water lines serve two small road sections beyond the neighborhood boundary. Attempts to include these road sections were made only after it was clear that additional members were necessary if the system was to be funded. Leaders of the dominant neighborhood did not directly contact residents outside their neighborhood but contacted leaders in outlying areas who in turn contacted residents in their areas. In a second system, one neighborhood was at the point of applying for a loan when an adjacent neighborhood which had not been successful in securing enough members requested that a consolidated system be designed to serve both communities. The first community agreed. Two years later, two additional adjacent neighborhoods joined the system through supplementary loans. These two additional neighborhoods also organized without direct assistance from members of neighborhoods already being served by the system.

In summary, three of the systems organized in Mississippi County serve a single neighborhood, one serves a single neighborhood and a section of another, and two serve multineighborhoods. In all these cases, organization took place within individual local neighborhoods, and in the case of multineighborhood systems was coordinated by leaders from each participating neighborhood. The only exception to this pattern of organization brought together fragments of two neighborhoods and an unorganized suburban housing area along a major highway. The leader in organizing this system was not a leader of a rural community but was more interested in suburban land development. (It is interesting that this is one of the two systems experiencing financial difficulty.)

Of the four systems currently in the planning stages, only one will serve a single rural neighborhood. It is impossible for this neighborhood to be joined by a larger system because of the location and design of completed systems surrounding it. Even this system will reach beyond its boundaries to take in rural residents who are not part of a recognized rural neighborhood. The other three projected systems all include three or more recognized rural neighborhoods, and in each case leaders in each separate neighborhood have been involved in preliminary plans.

Generalizing from this pattern, one can see three types of rural water systems in Mississippi: (1) those serving a single rural neighborhood, (2) those initially organized around a single rural neighborhood but with extensions into one or more adjacent rural neighborhoods, and (3) those initially organized around multiple rural neighborhoods. These three types of systems form an inexact but identifiable evolutionary pattern from smaller to larger units. Single neighborhood systems at first predominated in Mississippi County, but the current emphasis is on multineighborhood organization except where circumstances require smaller scale organization. Within all three types of systems, the single rural neighborhood predominates as the initial organizing unit.

It would be impossible to verify this pattern directly for the entire state without laboriously identifying local neighborhood boundaries in each of the state's eighty-two counties. However, informal interviewing of local FHA supervisors in other counties provides partial confirmation of the sequence described for Mississippi County. The major variation lies in the timing of initial organization of rural water systems in other counties. In counties in which systems were rapidly organized, there tends to be a greater proliferation of single-neighborhood systems and fewer multineighborhood systems. On the other hand, in counties in which initial organization of the first system was delayed, there are fewer single-neighborhood systems and a greater number of multineighborhood systems.

Analysis of statewide data on organized rural water systems also supports this general trend toward larger units. The average size water system funded shows a steady increase per year from 1963 to 1968, with the exception of a single year. The tendency to organize large systems is even more apparent than the increase in average system size. During the four-year period from 1963 to 1966, only five systems were organized serving two hundred or more members. But during 1967 and 1968, fifteen such systems were organized. This increase in size is even more apparent when the averages for the size of the initial system in each county are compared by year. Such a comparison seems to indicate that not only was the average size of funded systems increasing each year but FHA supervisors who delayed processing initial water system loans tended to benefit from the experience of other supervisors as to the liabilities of smaller systems.

The evolution of rural water systems in Mississippi was not complete with the shift in emphasis toward multineighborhood systems. Although the initial emphasis on larger-scale organization operated informally, the need for greater area planning in organization of water systems soon became formally recognized and resulted in a program of planning grants at the county level. These planning grants made possible detailed engineering studies of current status of water system development and the need for future development. The goal of these studies was to design the minimum number of additional systems to serve the maximum number of rural residents, regardless of local neighborhood boundaries.

There are other trends indicating that an increasing degree of centralization and coordination of water service will take place. Certain individuals and firms are now performing identical services such as billing, meter reading, and maintenance for more than one rural water system. Attempts are being made to organize these service functions for rural water systems on an area basis. Some county leaders are even envisioning the gradual development of area water service through either consolidation or, more likely, cooperation of individual water systems, both rural and urban. From a long-range point of view, the single rural neighborhood water system is only an intermediate stage between private wells in rural areas and larger water systems serving entire rural areas. In other states in which the individual rural neighborhood is less significant than in Mississippi and in which intensive participation in the rural water system program began at a later date, it seems that the stage of small neighborhood systems was largely bypassed with initial emphasis on larger area coverage.

While the nature of rural social organization affects the way in which rural water systems develop, the development of these systems in turn affects life in rural neighborhoods: it changes water consumption rates within households; it encourages the development of commercial farming operations; it changes the way in which rural landowners perceive the uses to which their land may be put; and while it may initially heighten the cohesiveness of the rural neighborhood, in the long run it lessens cohesiveness such that the rural neighborhood comes to resemble more nearly a residential suburb.

Changes in water use are most easily demonstrated in the case of lower-income families and larger commercial farming operations. As previously noted, rural water systems enabled many families who could not afford new wells to have a reliable source of safe water. However, this was not limited to individuals in the lower-income brackets, for many middle-income families delayed construction of new wells as long as possible by hauling drinking water during dry periods. During periods of water scarcity, many low- and middle-income families were forced to forgo activities which they would have undertaken with a more adequate water supply. As a result, the general consumption of water was drastically cut.

Spaulding (1967) found in a study of Warwick, Rhode Island, that social status varied directly with water consumption: higher-status households used more water than lower-status households. Since all the respondents in Spaulding's study had access to a community water supply, there was little question of nonavailability of water except for cases of extreme poverty. Yet, as we have seen, an individual well is a great expense for a small farmer or nonfarm laborer. Lack of money for well construction results in many families using less satisfactory wells, hauling water during time of water shortage, and delaying construction of wells whenever possible. Although data on individual consumption of water by household prior to construction of rural water systems are not available, interviewing in rural areas clearly indicates that there would be a great difference in water consumption between those who had deep wells and their neighbors who had less adequate wells, especially during summer and early fall. Since all rural water systems offer two to three thousand gallons of water per month for a minimum rate, an amount adequate for most rural nonfarm families, the differential in water use could be expected to be greatly reduced in rural areas with water systems. Socioeconomic status would in both cases be associated with higher water consumption, but the difference would be far less than when use of water depended on ability to construct and maintain a private water system. In other words, in rural areas with water systems the relationship of social status and water consumption would more nearly approximate that described for suburban areas.

Establishment of rural water systems has also been important in encouraging commercial farming operations. The two major forms of commercial farming operations requiring large quantities of safe water are poultry and dairying. Not only do these operations require large amounts of water, but loss of water supply for even a few days can result in a major financial loss. For example, some poultry operations are so large that it is very difficult to haul the necessary water for the flocks for several days while a pump is being repaired. Many of these commercial farmers have to maintain multiple wells as safeguards against loss of their water supply. The availability of a neighborhood water system enables such operators to keep their original wells as standby sources, while relying upon a water system for daily operations. In several rural neighborhoods larger commercial operators played a major role in organizing water systems, and their anticipated high uses of water made the systems more economically feasible. For the same reasons, commercial farm operators in some areas encouraged the establishment of large water systems with multiple wells so they could be assured adequate water even with the temporary failure of a single well in the system. In summary, we can conclude that rural water systems make possible a household water consumption pattern in rural areas more like that reported for suburban areas, and at the same time they facilitate the development and extension of large commercial farming operations.

Rural water systems have also had an impact on rural landowners' perception of land use. The cost of constructing private wells has already been discussed as a factor in the decision to leave a rural area and locate in a small town with a water system. Most rural residents mentioned the value of rural water systems in encouraging young people from the neighborhood to build new homes in the area and commute to nearby industrial jobs rather than build their homes in nearby towns. But at the same time, they recognized the financial advantage of rural water systems for any prospective home builder. As a result, the cost of land for home sites in rural areas served by rural water systems has greatly increased, with the increase being about half the cost of building a private well. Even so, many rural residents indicated a reluctance to sell land for individual home sites even at the increased price. Instead they are seeing the possibility of sub-division development in the future. In four of the seven areas served by water systems in Mississippi County, land has already been purchased for subdivision development. In some neighborhoods rural residents themselves have participated in this; in others, they are holding on to their land in anticipation of its increasing in value for home sites. In areas especially suitable for suburban development, many individuals are no longer speaking of stemming the migration of young people but rather of promoting growth of their community. Thus residents in rural neighborhoods, as a result of establishing a rural water system, begin to consider their land in nonagricultural terms. They begin to see possibilities of their rural community actually expanding in size and becoming increasingly composed of rural non-farm workers.

This brings us to a further area of impact of rural water systems, the impact of the organization and maintenance of the system on the rural neighborhood. We have seen that although the predominant unit for organization of the rural water system is the individual rural neighborhood, there has been an increasing tendency for single water systems to serve more than one rural neighborhood. As a result, there is a differential impact of water system organization on rural neighborhoods. Where the water system serves a single neighborhood, the process of organizing the water system tends to strengthen local leadership. The process of getting members of a community to organize a water association and then to follow through on the numerous details involved in securing a loan and operating the system requires a determined effort on the part of leaders within the neighborhood and cooperation from the majority of residents of the neighborhood. Additionally, in an age when rural post offices are being closed and rural schools are being consolidated, the water system is a visible sign of the continued existence of the rural neighborhood. This is especially true when the system is of sufficient size to justify an elevated water storage tank with the neighborhood name proudly proclaimed thereon. In fact, one of the obstacles to multineighborhood systems is their lack of neighborhood identification symbolized by the elevated tank of the single-neighborhood system. Since single-neighborhood systems tended to be organized in neighborhoods which previously had relatively strong neighborhood leadership and cooperation, the act of organizing the system could further facilitate the preservation of the individual neighborhood.

The opposite would seem to be true for rural neighborhoods involved in multineighborhood water systems. Here, the local neighborhood was generally weaker in leadership and common participation than were neighborhoods which organized independent systems. The act of organizing and operating multineighborhood systems requires the cooperation of leaders in separate rural neighborhoods. For this reason, the distinction between individual neighborhoods will probably decline in importance, and the possibility of other multineighborhood activities will be increased.

In the actual operation of water systems there is already a noticeable difference between single-neighborhood and multineighborhood systems. The small size of the single neighborhood permits operation on an informal basis, while larger multineighborhood systems are forced to adopt more formal patterns of operation. This can best be seen in the approach to collection of water bills. In the smaller system, the treasurer of the water system collects money from close friends and neighbors. As a result, informal social pressure can be used to encourage payment. The treasurer of one system found it quite effective to remind people publicly of their water bills while they were visiting with friends after church or in the neighborhood store. Few such public mentions of a bill were necessary before the bill was paid. The size of the multineighborhood system makes this pattern of informal operation more difficult. The leader of a system that had begun as a single-neighborhood system but had extended to three additional neighborhoods indicated that he was finally having to resort to stopping service when water bills became long overdue. He expressed concern that the water system was turning into a business operation, but he saw no way to avoid this. Also, maintenance and secretarial work in the single-neighborhood system is more likely to be undertaken as a volunteer service, at least in the early years of service, while multineighborhood systems more readily resort to paid maintenance and secretarial services. In both small and large systems, wide neighborhood participation tends to decrease, and with the passage of time most rural residents will come to view their water system as a public utility rather than a neighborhood-based association.

In fact, there is some indication that the change in perception of rural water systems from neighborhood association to public utility begins to occur even before the system is in operation. An older Mississippi farmer was explaining to me his difficulty in getting a water system funded. He was typical of older rural Mississippians, pronouncing Negro as "Nigger" and swearing that he would never call one of those "so and so's 'Mister.' " Yet when he could not get enough water users in his neighborhood, he contacted residents of an adjacent black farming neighborhood. Being unable to convince them personally of the value of the system, he contacted an NAACP leader in the county and asked him to organize the black neighborhood. Moreover, he later was instrumental in getting a black elected to the board of directors of the association. The system has not yet been constructed, and the farmer believes that there may be politics involved. He joked with me that if they did not get action soon, he might even talk with the NAACP about charging the FHA with discrimination against blacks. When in the process of organizing a water system, an older, quite prejudiced white Mississippi farmer can seek out and work with an NAACP leader and even joke about having other Mississippians charged with discrimination, it is clear that he has come to view the water system as a needed public utility rather than a neighborhood association.

I find the impact of rural water systems on rural neighborhoods particularly interesting since the initial organization of these systems was to a great degree in conformity with the existing social organization of rural neighborhoods. The lack of change agents promoting wider development resulted initially in organized systems serving rural neighborhoods and operating in an informal pattern characteristic of existing leadership patterns. Water-system development reflected both the constituency of the neighborhoods and leadership strengths of individual neighborhoods. However, both economic and organizational factors forced an evolution in scale of operation that is still expanding. These larger systems tend to be operated on a more business-like basis, and as a result the autonomy and identity of the individual rural neighborhood is weakened. Regardless of the size of the rural water system, the pattern of life in rural areas is changed: household water consumption more nearly approximates that of suburban areas; commercial farming operations are facilitated; land value increases for nonagricultural use; and the neighborhood comes to resemble more nearly a residential suburb. It seems that to the extent to which a program is successful in improving the quality of rural life and in perpetuating the existence of rural neighborhoods, it ultimately brings about the transformation of these neighborhoods.

NOTES

1. The work on which this paper is based was supported by a matching grant to the Social Science Research Center of Mississippi State University by the Office of Water Resources Research, United States Department of Interior, and the Mississippi Water Resources Research Institute as authorized under the Water Resources Act of 1964, Public Law 88–379. Further details about the methodology and results of this study are described in the project completion report (Peterson 1971). This project is part of a continuing research program in the Social Science Research Center and the Department of Sociology and Anthropology, Mississippi State University, dealing with behavioral aspects of natural resources problems and community development in rural areas.

2. Delineation of rural neighborhood boundaries and rating of leadership in rural neighborhoods of Mississippi County was developed by the author from unpublished data collected by Ben Barrentine and is on file at the Social Science Research Center, Mississippi State University. These data were collected under grant no. MH–1229 from the National Institute of Mental Health.

REFERENCES

Freeman, Charles, and Selz C. Mayo, 1957. Decision Makers in Rural Community Action. *Social Forces* 35:319-322.
Larson, Olaf F., and Everett M. Rogers, 1963. Rural Society in Transition: The American Setting. In *Our Changing Rural Society: Perspectives and Trends*, James H. Copp, ed. (Ames, Iowa: Iowa State University Press), pp. 39-67.
Peterson, John H., Jr., 1971. *Community Organization and Rural Water System Development* (State College, Miss.: Mississippi State University, Water Resources Research Institute).
Spaulding, Irving A., 1967. *Household Water Use and Social Status*. Bulletin 392: (Kingston: University of Rhode Island, Agricultural Experiment Station).
United States Department of Agriculture, 1963. *Century of Service* (Washington, D.C.: GPO).
──────, 1968. *Report of the Secretary of Agriculture* (Washington, D.C.: GPO).

The Morality of Applied Anthropology

JOHN J. HONIGMANN

WE are in a period when anthropology, along with the other social sciences, is undergoing intense moral examination. What marks this self-criticism will leave on our discipline, and how lasting those marks will be, we must wait and see. The fact that ethical concerns are being pressed most strongly by younger members of the profession, including students now undergoing professional preparation, suggests that a number of anthropologists will continue for many years to be worried about the moral aspects of the discipline and therefore concerned with finding safeguards against undesirable practices.

My paper is limited to the ethics of professionally trained anthropologists vis-à-vis directed culture change. I have assumed that anthropologists who have things of practical significance to say about directed change are generally well-intentioned and responsible men and women. By "well-intentioned" I mean that they will not allow themselves to be employed if they know that the evil they may do will very likely outweigh the good. Naturally there is bound to be variation in opinions of this kind from one professional person to another. By "responsible" I mean that anthropologists reflect on the nature and goals of a task before they accept a commission and that they feel concern for their limited ability to predict and control the consequences of their acts. Because they are far from omniscient, anthropologists know the importance of reflection and concern in what they do; hence the pertinence of ethics for guiding them. I would probably have written quite a different paper if I had started by assuming that anthropologists generally allow themselves to be hired to help in callously carrying out acts that they believe to be irreversibly evil.[1]

It may be well to begin by describing my personal involvement in applied anthropology, my attitudes toward directed culture change, and how those attitudes took shape.

Early in my career as a graduate student, which coincided with the start of World War II, I recall maintaining that anthropology should only be a theoretical or a pure science. I have mentioned the war, and I should also explain that I was then a firmly committed pacifist. I saw that a number of anthropologists were going to work for military agencies at that time, but my memory and personal papers are not good enough to enable me to know if my attitude toward applied anthropology stemmed basically from my pacificism.

In my second year of graduate school, after I had returned from my first fieldwork with the Athapaskan Indians of northwestern Canada, I wrote articles trying to persuade Canadian authorities to improve the welfare of those Indians (Honigmann 1943, 1943-1944, 1944). I am sure that, being inspired with the desire to help the Indians, I did not realize that I was also urging culturally disturbing intervention in their lives, something I specifically repudiated. Or perhaps I did vaguely realize it, since my recommendations also called for preserving the cultural status quo by halting further dissolution of the traditional cultures. In an article published in 1943, I also praised John Collier, then commissioner of Indian affairs, for having ended (as I then thought) the autocratic phase of United States Indian policy.

I realize now how inconsistent my position was. I wanted the Canadian government to improve conditions among the Indians, but I wanted their culture left alone as much as possible. Today I take the view that the effects of intervention in a social system cannot be precisely limited to designated areas and kept from spilling over into other areas or having widely ramifying consequences. To say that a culture or a society is a system means what it says: inputs in one area of life are bound to have ramifications in other areas.

My second involvement in applied anthropology came in 1946, while I was holding my first teaching job. An ad hoc Canadian committee comprised of medical men and an anthropologist invited me to study the food ways of a group of Canadian Indians. I accepted without hesitation. Reviewing my correspondence I am reminded that I was as much—if not more—attracted to this task by the prospect of spending a whole year among people in the Far North (I had grown very fond of the area and its people) as I was attracted by the applied nature of the research. The study that I was asked to do was based on two premises: first, that the hunting and collecting Indians of Canada were suffering from malnutrition and, second, that instituting change in diet was not a medical but a social problem requiring adequate "sociological" information. The anthropological coordinator of the project, G. Gordon Brown, was a British-trained social anthropologist: hence the reference to "sociological" information. Brown was also one of the first to do applied work in our discipline. I accepted the committee's offer, confidently expecting that the investigation would bring benefits to the people of the region.

The research was carried out among Cree Indians in Attawapiskat, Ontario, and in 1948 I wrote a report that concluded with several recommendations designed for an action program that would seek to increase native self-sufficiency (Honigmann 1962). In those recommendations I no longer spoke about preserving the cultural status quo, although I was still manifestly undecided on the question of how much and what kind of change was good for an exotic culture. I recommended developing the native culture along directions it had for many years been following. For example, I urged that help be offered to the Cree Indians to enable them more effectively to solve problems arising from their way of life and their habitat. I reasoned that just as agricultural research had brought tremendous improvements to European and United States farming, so research and development undertaken in Eurocanadian culture could improve the technical aspects of northern Algonkian culture and bring about a better way of life for those people. Consequently the Indian culture would not become more and more an imitation of the white man's, but would be brought to a point of richer potential without being divorced from tradition (Honigmann 1951-1952).

I have since parted company with the attitude of gradualism and the infatuation with tradition that those recommendations embody, thanks largely to the influence of Margaret Mead's book, *New Lives for Old,* and my subsequent experience in other parts of the Canadian North. Increasingly, my sympathy grew for the aims of directed culture change. It grew, for example, as I studied community development in Pakistan and contemplated its organization in other countries (Swezey and Honigmann 1962). But mainly it was through observing the transformation of Eskimo life, accomplished among those Eskimo who were being accommodated in an eastern Arctic government-planned town, that I came to perceive the advantages of directed culture change in massive doses. Large-scale culture change in the Arctic has done much to augment native people's physical welfare and to promote their adaptation into the modern world with whose political and other institutions their lives are already enmeshed (Honigmann 1970).

Now to turn to the subject indicated by the title of this essay: problems of conscience or morality arising in applied anthropology.

To begin, let us remind ourselves of the way moral judgments are achieved. The good or evil we impute to a particular program of directed culture change, or to directed culture change in general, cannot be derived from previous experiments in applied anthropology or from the history of programs of directed culture change that went on before. At best, experimentation and history may help predict the outcome of a particular program, but they do not tell us whether directed change or its expected outcomes are good or bad.

Moral judgments are not primarily based on facts. Moral judgments arise through imputing an attribute to facts or to expectations that the facts and expectations themselves do not possess. To be sure, the good or evil we attribute to a program of directed culture change or its probable outcomes may be influenced by the facts of previous work in anthropology. Nevertheless, good and evil are ultimately personal judgments, and even though they are shaped by the moral values shared in the society where our personal judgments are made, there exists much room for divergent moral opinions even in the same society.

Students in anthropology, undergraduate and graduate, frequently ask whether it is right for anthropologists to lend their talents to interfering in another way of life by deliberately inducing changes in it. As a teacher I try to avoid giving a categorical or authoritative "yes" or "no" answer to such a question. Pedagogically speaking, a categorical answer is unwise because it deprives the questioner of an opportunity to reach a decision by himself. In the language of the code adopted by the Society for Applied Anthropology in 1949, answering such questions authoritatively might undermine the potentiality for change in an individual through which his greater well-being might be achieved.

But there is another reason which is not primarily pedagogical, for refraining from a categorical answer. Obviously several answers are possible to such a question. Troubled by the morality of directed culture change in general, or by the morality of some particular program of directed culture change, an individual will normally reach a decision on the basis of the values generally endorsed in the society and groups to which he belongs, personal factors deriving from his individual life history, and his current motivational status. To put it in other terms, one's moral decisions are influenced by the historical situation in which one lives (see Maquet 1964). The historical situation includes the future as far as one can visualize it or, more specifically, the probable outcome of the line of action from the standpoint of the person contemplating it. The refusal to give a categorical answer to a complex question involving a moral dimension recognizes that several answers are possible and allows an individual to decide a course of action in terms of his personal historical situation. The alternative would be to offer an answer best suited to the historical situation of someone else.

My reluctance to state a categorical position for another person with respect to the morality of directed culture change does not mean that I personally hold no standards for judging my own and other people's participation in such activity. I do hold such standards, and I am quite willing to discuss them with others, though without any thought that they are impregnable or necessarily binding under any and all conditions. For example, I generally favor allowing members of a social system or social category to practice their beliefs and values and to retain their culture, but I can easily conceive of cases when I would support action that would limit certain cultural practices in another social system, no matter how strongly they were valued by the people concerned.

I am more confident about the general applicability of the ethic in the 1949 Code of the Society for Applied Anthropology, which states that no intervention into another social system should be undertaken if one knows that such intervention will set in motion a train of events involving irreversible loss of health or life or create irreversible damage to the natural productivity of the physical environment.[2]

Also I believe that someone who participates in directed culture change should, in the language of the society's code (see also Mead 1955: chap. 6), be concerned "either with maintaining a system of human relationships in a state of dynamic equilibrium or in aiding the resolution of a system into such a new state as to achieve a greater degree of well-being for the constituent individuals. He is [also] concerned with preserving within such a state of equilibrium those potentialities for change through which greater well-being for the individual can be achieved." Of course, much debate can ensue in trying to decide what are valid empirical indicators of equilibrium states and, in the absence of good experimental data, when a particular program of directed culture change furthers those states. But those matters need not be taken up here.

Credo is only credo; a credo is not a set of rules binding on me or anybody under conditions that cannot yet be foreseen. And someone reasoning logically from different premises might reach conclusions quite different from the SAA code. I would want that to be fully understood by anyone asking about the morality of applied anthropology.

Although moral and ethical judgments, whether made by an individual or an association, are always reached in a particular historical situation, they are not wholly relativistic. Such judgments are always limited by the cultural values of the society in which they are formed and by the social pressure exercised or threatened in that society or in its component professional groups. On the other hand culture and social pressure do not utterly determine behavior; they merely limit it, thereby reducing the probability of novelty. It is always possible to transcend the limits set by culture and society and to innovate comparatively new conceptions of morality under specific conditions, and I for one wish to maintain generous limits of tolerance for such innovation that might be made by a responsible person confronting conditions that cannot now be foreseen.

For the same reason that I am reluctant to offer categorical advice concerning the morality of culture change, I am opposed to professional codes of ethics in anthropology that are more than guidelines or that have punitive sanctions attached to them. Professional ethical codes are well-intentioned but give a misleading impression of fixity and universal applicability; and this is especially true of those backed by sanctions. Durability and generality should not be expected from injunctions devised in a profession like ours. In the first place, any code contains only the judgments of the small number of persons who drafted it and who, however wise they may have been, were individually bound by their own, individual historical situations. What is even more important, codes are bound to run up against the realities of a culturally heterogeneous society in which, whether we like it or not, diversity and innovation are encouraged and flourish.

In a small, culturally homogeneous society any person's judgment is far more likely to reflect concurrence with the attitudes of other people than is the case in a large heterogeneous society where immensely different experiences, values, and attitudes distinguish individuals, groups, and categories. Consequently, there is much scope in a heterogeneous society for any person's moral judgment to be at variance with the moral judgment of others and to be regarded as immoral by others. Even members of a single profession may hold widely divergent standards. In other words, a member of a heterogeneous society must expect a plural number of moral judgments, even moral judgments in conflict with one another.

Other modern professions, such as the bar, have codes with enforcement procedures. I found it interesting to read in a recent study of lawyers' ethics that few unethical lawyers are caught or punished by the formal disciplinary machinery of the bar (Carlin 1966). Only the more visible offenses of lawyers are dealt with by the enforcement procedure. Hence, rather than functioning to punish wrongdoing and so protect the public, the controls of the bar serve primarily to forestall public criticism of the legal profession by taking action in those cases where the public becomes aware of some notoriously unethical act.

I have heard the same function given as an argument for an ethical code and punitive sanctions binding on anthropology. If individual anthropologists do things that most of us dislike, the argument runs, the profession as a whole will come into bad repute, and we may lose the opportunity to do certain kinds of research. A code or system of sanctions will provide the profession with a means of reaffirming its disapprobation, the argument continues, perhaps by reading the offender out of anthropology, thereby making the public aware of the ethical sentiments of the majority.

Rather than get into the debate of whether or not it is meritorious to protect one's profession—doing what Radcliffe-Brown might call maintaining the continuity of the social system of anthropology—we ought to recognize the extent to which formal sanctions threaten to substitute conformity for morality. Sanctions are relatively unconcerned with resolving moral questions. When they threaten to penalize behavior that does not confirm the existing code—whatever the reason for such nonconformity—they actually discourage the debate of moral issues.

To be sure, there is danger in directed culture change, particularly when—as is usually the case—it is undertaken with respect to subject people who are comparatively powerless to resist and who are not advised of their right to resist—if indeed they are acknowledged to have that right. The way to control such abuses is for professional organizations to encourage the widest publicity for programs of directed culture change, especially when anthropologists are employed in them, and thereby maintain a strong public opinion at a high state of alertness within the profession.

Meetings and symposia organized by anthropological societies are one means whereby programs of directed culture change could receive publicity and their moral implications could be explored and debated. Discussion promoted through such meetings might go far in cultivating and sharpening our sense of professional morality with respect to directed culture change, whether it is undertaken by anthropologists themselves or by other agencies whose work the anthropologist reviews. In such discussion we would test the logic on which our moral standards are founded. A person reporting on his own work in applied anthropology might be challenged not only on the adequacy of his research and recommendation but on the morality of his undertaking. Such debate would sometimes confirm one in his moral wisdom, but it could promote moral reflection that would also shake one's original convictions. Even members of the audience could undergo an experience that would contribute toward the formation of new value notions. Let anthropological societies foster such exchanges bearing on ethical questions rather than design codes that incorporate frozen, situationally bound moral norms. Thereby the self-criticism that anthropology is undergoing today will continue to be a stimulus to moral reflection about our discipline.

NOTES

1. For comments on an earlier and very brief version of this paper I am grateful to Lawrence Hall, Steven Polgar, and Frances Ferguson.
2. The Statement of Ethics of the Society for Applied Anthropology (1963-1964) is even more general and easy to accept, though less thought-provoking than the 1949 code.

REFERENCES

Carlin, Jerome E., 1966. *Lawyers' Ethics* (New York: Russell Sage Foundation).
Honigmann, John J., 1943. White Man's New Burden. *Commonweal* 37:511-514.
————, 1943-1944. On the Alaska Highway. *Dalhousie Review* 23:400-408.
————, 1944. Canada's Human Resources. *Canadian Forum* 24:84.
————, 1951-1952. The Logic of the James Bay Survey. *Dalhousie Review* 30:377-386.
————, 1962. *Foodways in a Muskeg Community.* Northern Co-ordination and Research Centre, Department of Indian Affairs and Northern Development, publication 62:1.
————, 1965. *Eskimo Townsmen.* Canadian Research Centre for Anthropology (Ottawa: St. Paul University).
———— , 1970. Education in the Modernization of Cultures. *Transactions of the Sixth World Congress of Sociology,* vol. 3.
Maquet, J. J., 1964. Objectivity in Anthropology. *Current Anthropology* 5:47-55.
Mead, M., ed., 1955. *Cultural Patterns and Technical Change* (Paris: UNESCO).
Society for Applied Anthropology, 1949. Report of the Committee on Ethics. *Human Organization* 8:20–21.
————, 1963-1964. Statement on Ethics of the Society for Applied Anthropology. *Human Organization* 22:237.
Swezey, F. Curtiss, and John J. Honigmann, 1962. The Origins of Community Development. *International Review of Community Development* 10:165–176.

The Contributors

Joseph B. Aceves is assistant professor of anthropology at Southern Methodist University. Author of two books on social change in Spain, he has also done fieldwork among Hispanic populations in the United States. His major research interests are in the areas of changing values and world views, and rural development programs in complex societies.

Wilfrid C. Bailey is professor of anthropology and sociology in the Department of Sociology and Anthropology at the University of Georgia. His major research interests have been in community studies, change and development, and the anthropology of education.

Elizabeth A. Brandt is assistant professor of anthropology in the Department of Anthropology at the University of Illinois at Chicago Circle. Her major interests are southwestern ethnology, ethnolinguistics, and cognitive anthropology. She has done field research on rapid linguistic change and multilingualism.

John J. Honigmann is professor of anthropology at the University of North Carolina, Chapel Hill. His research has been centered mainly in the subarctic region of Canada with additional fieldwork in West Pakistan and rural Austria. He also studied a Strategic Air Command Bomber Squadron.

Arden R. King is professor and head of the Department of Anthropology, Newcomb College, and research associate of the Middle American Research Institute in Tulane University. His primary interests are in Nuclear America (especially Meso-America) and anthropological theory. He has recently done field research in northern Germany.

James L. Peacock is associate professor and associate chairman in the Department of Anthropology, University of North Carolina, Chapel Hill. His main interest is in the ideological and psychological

111

112 *Aspects of Cultural Change*

dimensions of modernization. Among his publications is *The Human Direction*, with A. Thomas Kirsch, a cultural anthropology text from an evolutionary viewpoint.

John H. Peterson, Jr., is assistant professor in the Department of Sociology and Anthropology and assistant anthropologist in the Social Science Research Center at Mississippi State University. His research interests include ethnohistory, contemporary community, minority relations, and applied anthropology in education and natural resources development.

Miles Richardson is associate professor of anthropology and chairman of the Department of Geography and Anthropology, Louisiana State University, Baton Rouge. His principal interest is in contemporary cultures of Spanish America, particularly the material environment of town and small city life. He has done fieldwork in Columbia and Costa Rica.

Ben J. Wallace is associate professor of anthropology at Southern Methodist University. His primary research interest is agricultural change in Southeast Asia and his most recent book is *Village Life in Insular Southeast Asia*. His paper on rural hippie communes is a result of research conducted in northern New Mexico where in the summers of 1970 and 1971 he was director of SMU's field school in ethnology.

. . . we are a process of becoming, fitting together and falling apart. It changes and we change and it changes . . .

OTHER SOUTHERN ANTHROPOLOGICAL SOCIETY PROCEEDINGS